PUBLISHERS

Commercial Real Estate Transactions Handbook
Third Edition

Edited by Mark A. Senn

Commercial Real Estate Transactions Handbook is an invaluable reference that explores all sides of real estate transactions from contracts and financing to arrangements and leases. This comprehensive resource provides subscribers with analysis and coverage of today's important topics, including environmental concerns and liabilities, the Americans with Disabilities Act, the Lender Liability Rule, and much more. In addition, this book contains ready-to-use forms and checklists, as well as new insights on broker agreements, commercial real estate leases, and real estate in bankruptcy.

Highlights of the 2004 Cumulative Supplement

The 2004 Cumulative Supplement expands the scope of the main volume to provide essential new information:

- New section discussing the problems and effect of mold as they relate to construction contracts.

- Enhanced discussion of model opinion letters and bar committee reports.

- New section discussing standardization of opinion letters versus "customary practice."

- Expanded discussion of the Brownfields Revitalization and Environmental Restoration Act, which clarified the innocent landowner defense to CERCLA.

- New section discussing government led insurance incentive programs designed to foster the use of environmental insurance to stimulate the cleanup and redevelopment of brownfield sites.

- New Forms, including:

- Alternative to current Form 12-3 for Basic Rent Provisions— Statement of Estimated Expense Charges Included;

- Form 12-4A, Limit on Increases in Controllable Operating Expenses.

- Variety of new cases from different jurisdictions addressing issues arising in the area of common interest ownership.

The Index is also updated to reflect all changes to the text.

6/04

For questions concerning this shipment, billing, or other customer service matters, call our Customer Service Department at 1-800-234-1660.

For toll-free ordering, please call 1-800-638-8437.

A WoltersKluwer Company

COMMERCIAL REAL ESTATE TRANSACTIONS HANDBOOK

2004 Cumulative Supplement

This supplement supersedes all previous supplements.

COMMERCIAL REAL ESTATE TRANSACTIONS HANDBOOK
THIRD EDITION

2004 Cumulative Supplement

MARK A. SENN
Editor

PUBLISHERS

1185 Avenue of the Americas, New York, NY 10036
www.aspenpublishers.com

This publication is designed to provide accurate and authoritative information in regard to the subject matter covered. It is sold with the understanding that the publisher is not engaged in rendering legal, accounting, or other professional services. If legal advice or other professional assistance is required, the services of a competent professional person should be sought.

—From a *Declaration of Principles* jointly adopted
by a Committee of the American Bar Association
and a Committee of Publishers and Associations

© 2004 Aspen Publishers, Inc.
A Wolters Kluwer Company
www.aspenpublishers.com

Printed in the United States of America

1 2 3 4 5 6 7 8 9 0

Library of Congress Cataloging-in-Publication Data

Commercial real estate transactions handbook / [edited by] Mark Senn. — 3rd ed.
   p. cm.
   Rev. ed. of: Negotiating and structuring real estate transactions. 2nd ed. c1993.
   Includes index.
   ISBN 0-7355-0573-X
   ISBN 0-7355-4717-3 (supplement)
      1. Vendors and purchasers — United States. 2. Real estate development — Law and legislation United States. 3. Mortgages — United States. 4. Commercial leases — United States. I. Senn, Mark A. II. Negotiating and structuring real estate transactions.

KF665 .C575 2000
346.7304'37 dc21   00-038037

About Aspen Publishers

Aspen Publishers, headquartered in New York City, is a leading information provider for attorneys, business professionals, and law students. Written by preeminent authorities, our products consist of analytical and practical information covering both U.S. and international topics. We publish in the full range of formats, including updated manuals, books, periodicals, CDs, and online products.

Our proprietary content is complemented by 2,500 legal databases, containing over 11 million documents, available through our Loislaw division. Aspen Publishers also offers a wide range of topical legal and business databases linked to Loislaw's primary material. Our mission is to provide accurate, timely, and authoritative content in easily accessible formats, supported by unmatched customer care.

To order any Aspen Publishers title, go to *www.aspenpublishers.com* or call 1-800-638-8437.

To reinstate your manual update service, call 1-800-638-8437.

For more information on Loislaw products, go to *www.loislaw.com* or call 1-800-364-2512.

For Customer Care issues, e-mail CustomerCare@aspenpublishers.com; call 1-800-234-1660; or fax 1-800-901-9075.

Aspen Publishers
A Wolters Kluwer Company

CONTENTS

Sections listed below appear only in the supplement and not in the main volume.

Chapter 11
ENVIRONMENTAL ISSUES IN COMMERCIAL
REAL ESTATE SALES AND LEASES **105**

Chapter 12
INDUSTRIAL LEASES... **131**

Chapter 14
OFFICE LEASES... **139**

Chapter 15
ASSIGNMENT OF LEASES **143**

Chapter 16
COMMON INTEREST OWNERSHIP.................................. **151**

Chapter 17
BANKRUPTCY **163**

CHAPTER 4

CONSTRUCTION CONTRACTS

Philip E. Beck

---

§ 4.02 CONTRACT STRUCTURE: CHOOSING A CONTRACTUAL RELATIONSHIP

[E] Design/Build

Page 147, add at end of subsection [E]:

Due to its increasing popularity in recent years, and projections by construction industry insiders that this trend will continue in the decade ahead, design/build is discussed in greater detail in **§§ 4.09[A]** through **[G]** of this supplement.

Page 205, add new sections at end of chapter:

§ 4.09 THE DESIGN/BUILD MOVEMENT

[A] Growth of Design/Build

In **§ 4.02[E]** of the main volume, design/build construction was introduced as one of the four common construction contracting structures, or "project delivery systems." "Design/build," as that phrase is used in the construction industry, denotes the situation in which the owner of a project contracts with a single entity to both design the project and construct the project in accordance with that design. Thus, the owner who selects this project delivery system needs to look only to a single source for both design and construction.

The design/builder may be a company possessing both design and construction capabilities in-house; it may be a general contractor who, in turn, hires an architect/engineer to design the project, operating essentially as a subcontractor to the design/builder; it may, in some states,[128] be

1

an architect/engineer who, in turn, hires a contractor to construct its design; or it may be a joint venture (a partnership formed for the limited purpose of performing a specific project) composed of one or more design firms plus one or more construction firms.

Use of the design/build project delivery system has increased exponentially over the past two decades, with design/build quickly becoming the project delivery system of choice in the United States and throughout the world. Estimates indicate that by the mid-1990s design/build accounted for ten times the construction volume it accounted for just 10 years earlier. Many predict that by 2010 design/build will account for 50 percent of the nonresidential construction market in the United States. Perhaps more impressive, design/build is rapidly becoming the preferred method of project delivery in the public sector, as well as the private sector. This is true despite the fact that competitive bidding laws in many states had to be rewritten before many public owners could utilize design/build.[129]

[B] History of Design/Build

Like many "new" ideas, design/build is actually the rebirth of an old one. The modern-day design/builders closely resemble the "master builders" of yesteryear, who built the wondrous pyramids of Egypt, the Great Wall of China, and India's Taj Mahal. Obviously, construction techniques have changed a great deal since those ancient projects were constructed, and most modern-day construction projects do not take hundreds of years to complete. Yet the underlying philosophy that it is better to simplify the contract structure by having a single point of responsibility and accountability for both design and construction is as sound today as it was then. Thus, the use of the design/build project delivery approach, for appropriate projects, truly does reflect "the wisdom of the ages."

Moreover, advocates of design/build argue that the inherent benefits of design/build are even more relevant today than they were in the days of old. The modern-day construction process involves legal, regulatory, environmental, societal, technological, economic, financial, market-related, timing, and other challenges and constraints that the master builders of yore could not have even imagined. Out of this greater complexity comes an even greater need to simplify the process by unifying responsibilities.

[C] Advantages of Design/Build

The remarkable growth in the popularity of design/build in recent years is evidence of the fact that owners of construction projects perceive its advantages to outweigh its disadvantages, at least for many projects. Some of the major advantages of design/build include:

1. The single point of design and construction responsibility characteristic of design/build shifts the risks of design deficiencies and conflicts between the designer and the contractor from the owner to the design/builder, resulting in less project risk for the owner.

2. Design/build tends to produce a shorter "time to market" and to better facilitate "fast track" construction (i.e., construction that proceeds as design work is still being performed). Studies have suggested that design/build projects are approximately one-third faster than traditional "design—then bid—then build" projects and approximately one-fourth faster than projects utilizing a "construction manager at-risk" (a construction manager with schedule and budget responsibility). In today's world, such time savings can be of critical importance.

3. Design/build tends to provide greater predictability and control of both the project schedule and the project budget, due to the consolidation of design and construction responsibility and accountability.

4. Design/build allows both the contractor and the designer to be actively involved in the project from the very early stages, providing the owner the benefit of both disciplines' input in the early project planning and design.

5. Design/build tends to promote greater cooperation, coordination, and teamwork between the contractor and the designer, and within the entire project team, and to result in less "finger pointing" between the contractor and the designer.

6. Design/build typically reduces the owner's administrative burden and produces less frustration and aggravation for the owner.

7. Design/build usually breeds fewer claims, disputes, and lawsuits than other project delivery systems.

[D]   Disadvantages of Design/Build

Like everything in life, design/build involves certain trade-offs. Some of the major disadvantages of design/build are:

1. With the lower risk that is characteristic of design/build may come less control and less reward, as more decisions are left to the discretion of the design/builder.

2. The consolidation of design and construction responsibility under a single entity removes the "checks and balances" system that exists when the designer and the contractor are separate, autonomous entities, both working for the owner. This factor alone causes some owners to reject design/build for fear that "the fox would be guarding the hen house" and that problems would be "swept under the rug."

3. The contractor selection process is both costly and time-consuming with design/build.

4. For public owners particularly, design/build procurement may be difficult or complicated, or it may not be legally permissible.

5. By vesting more power and responsibility in the design/builder, some feel the owner has less quality assurance and quality control.[130]

6. Under design/build, the owner relinquishes some of its control and flexibility in developing the design of the project. If an owner wishes to micro-manage the design process and make continuous changes to the design, the promise of greater budget control and schedule control becomes illusory.

7. Because it is still new to some, participants in the design/build process sometimes do not fully understand their roles and responsibilities, which can lead to problems. In addition, the insurance policies carried by many design and construction firms, as well as state licensing laws, may not be compatible with the characteristics of design/build.

[E]   Selecting the Right Project Delivery System

An owner should consider a number of factors in deciding which of the available project delivery systems is best suited to that owner and the particular project involved. Design/build works better for some owners and some types of projects than for others. Some of the factors an owner should consider when selecting a project delivery system include:

1. Are there legal or political requirements or considerations (such as public procurement laws and state licensing laws)?

2. How critical is the project schedule?

3. How critical is the project budget?

4. How well defined are the owner's needs?

5. How complex is the project?

6. What are the capabilities, sophistication, and experience of each of the parties?

7. How much control does the owner desire/can the owner handle?

8. How much do the parties trust one another?

Both logic and experience suggest that design/build is best suited for certain types of projects. Among these are projects in which the owner's needs and requirements are clearly defined at the outset, projects involving the repetition of prior design and construction (such as fast-food chain restaurants), projects in which less owner input is desired and required, projects driven by performance needs rather than aesthetics (such as manufacturing facilities), projects in which "time to market" is critical (such as a manufacturing plant required to bring a new product to market quickly), and projects for owners who are particularly risk-averse.

[F] Ramifications of Selection for Roles, Relationships, Rights, and Responsibilities

Regardless of whether the project delivery system chosen for a particular project is design/build or one of the other alternatives, it is imperative to the success of a project that the project participants fully understand their respective roles, the relationships of their roles to one another, and their respective rights and responsibilities. Each contract structure carries with it a unique set of party roles and relationships and creates a unique set of rights and responsibilities. In order to assess and manage the risks inherent in every construction project, the parties should make sure they know, and agree upon, who is responsible, and to what extent, for each of the following:

1. Suitability of the design;

2. Design changes;

3. Coordination of contractors;

4. Control of the schedule;

5. Control of the budget;

6. Unforeseen subsurface conditions;

7. Changes in market conditions;

8. Any loss of productivity;

9. Unanticipated schedule impacts; and

10. The unexpected.

Owners, contractors, and designers who are new to design/build are sometimes surprised at some of their responsibilities. For example, contractors are not accustomed to being accountable to the owner for the suitability of the project design, as they are under design/build. This is the complete opposite of the *Spearin* doctrine, discussed in **§ 4.03[C][1],** at pages 151–153 of the main volume. Contractors also typically assume far greater risks with respect to unanticipated subsurface site conditions under design/build construction than with other project delivery systems.

[G]   Making Design/Build Work

As with any construction project, the biggest key to a successful design/build project is to select the right project team. If an owner is fortunate enough to select a good design/builder who is experienced in projects of the type involved, possesses the requisite expertise, is dedicated to working as a member of the team to make the project a success, and will dedicate the right mix of capable personnel and company resources to the project, the project is well on its way to being a success. While the selection of the best contract structure for a particular project is important, the selection of the right people to fill in the boxes on the organizational chart is even more so. This may be even more critical under the design/build project delivery approach than under other contracting structures.

Part of the trick to selecting the right project participants is implementing an appropriate selection process. Selection of a design/builder generally should be a two-step process consisting of a prequalification phase, during which the initial list of candidates is reduced to a "short list," and a final selection phase, during which the design/builder for the project is selected from the design/builders who made the short list. As noted previously, the selection process for a design/build project can be very costly, complicated, and time-consuming. It is imperative, however, that the owner use a reasonable, but thorough, selection process. To avoid any unnecessary costs, the owner should generally require minimal design documentation to be submitted during the prequalification phase, focusing more on the qualifications of the candidates and their compatibility with the owner and the project. The owner should also seriously consider paying each of the unsuccessful candidates who made the short list a stipend to help defray the costs necessarily incurred in pursuing the project and to partially compensate them for their contributions to the project.

Once the design/builder is selected, and as part of the selection process itself, the owner should develop and implement a good design/build contract that clearly defines each party's rights and responsibilities and clearly allocates project risks. The Associated General Contractors of America has developed a good set of design/build contract forms that have been endorsed by owners, contractors, and designers alike. These can be used in lieu of a customized contract if the project budget will not support one or can be used as a starting point in preparing a contract tailored to the unique needs of a specific project.

As suggested previously, if the project is to be successful, it is important for the project participants to fully identify and understand each party's rights and responsibilities and to recognize, allocate, and manage the various risks inherent in any construction project. All of the parties must also be committed to using the design/build process, to working together as a team, and to achieving the project's objectives.

For design/build to work as intended, it is imperative that the owner provide the design/builder, at the outset, a clear statement of the owner's program requirements, with the scope and intent of the project defined in sufficient detail to avoid any miscommunication and the disputes miscommunication can cause. The owner should also implement appropriate monitoring and quality assurance procedures throughout the project to ensure that both design and construction are progressing as envisioned.

If the right project team is assembled and the right procedures are put in place and adhered to, design/build can provide an excellent vehicle for achieving a successful project.

---

[128] In some states, such as North Carolina, current laws require that the entity holding the contract with the owner be a licensed general contractor. This effectively

precludes "architect-led" design/build construction in those states, requiring "contractor-led" design/build instead.

[129] Almost by definition, when multiple bidders (or offerors) are competing for a design/build project, they are submitting prices based upon somewhat different projects, i.e., each bidder's unique design. Accordingly, design/build does not lend itself to selecting a contractor based upon the traditional competitive bidding process, where price is the only determinant, because "apples to apples" comparison is not possible. Even in the public sector, the selection of a design/builder must be based, in part, on subjective factors. In many states, new public procurement legislation had to be enacted in order to allow public owners this flexibility in the contractor selection process.

[130] Advocates of design/build, however, point to studies indicating that design/build actually produces a higher-quality project.

§ 4.10   MOLD: WHAT YOU NEED TO KNOW BEFORE YOU NEED TO KNOW IT*

[A]   Mold: The Construction Industry's Newest Four-Letter Word

The latest "curse" upon the construction industry is *mold*. Mold claims, disputes, and litigation are growing like ... well, like mold. Many have predicted that mold will even surpass asbestos as a source of construction claims and disputes and a subject of multi-million dollar litigation. The threat of mold, and its potential consequences, *should* impact how today's owners/developers, design professionals, and construction professionals: select, locate, plan, execute, budget for, contract for, design, engineer, specify, procure, construct, staff, train for, supervise, inspect, administer, schedule, sequence, insure, manage, complete, test, commission, operate, maintain, present, portray, and publicize their projects. In short, thoughts of mold and its potential (real or imagined) health, legal, societal, political, and economic ramifications should permeate every aspect of the design and construction process—not as a paralyzing paranoia, but as an impetus to proactive planning.

[1]   Why All the Fuss?

While there is still a great divergence of opinions as to the magnitude of the health risk involved, and even whether mold poses any health risk at all, there is now substantial medical and scientific evidence to suggest

---

* This section is prepared by Philip E. Beck and Sarah E. Carson of Smith, Currie & Hancock, LLP. © 2004 Smith, Currie & Hancock LLP.

that extended exposure to at least certain types of mold can be injurious to humans. The frequent occurrence of mold during or as a result of the construction process, combined with the potential health risks and a heightened public awareness of the risk, has created a breeding ground for litigation and the risks, costs, and uncertainty that litigation entails.

[2] Omnipotent or Just Omnipresent?

Mold is everywhere. The United States Environmental Protection Agency (EPA) has concluded that all molds can cause health problems under certain conditions.[1] However, it seems undisputed that some molds pose more of a health risk than others. How much of a health risk each poses remains open to debate.

[3] Toxic or Non-Toxic?

The term *toxic mold* has become part of the modern lexicon of construction terms. It is actually the media, however — not the medical or scientific communities — that has coined the phrase "toxic mold," because, frankly, the term "toxic" sells. The phrase typically is used, if used as presumably intended, to refer to any mold that produces "toxic" compounds. The Centers for Disease Control has recognized 25 "toxic molds" out of the several thousands of identified molds.[2] Many of these toxic molds can enter the body through skin contact or inhalation.[3] The most publicized of these toxic molds is *stachybotrys chartarum* or "black mold," which usually covers the inside walls of buildings.[4] *Stachybotrys chartarum* was documented as early as 60 years ago when neurological disorders and related illnesses causing the deaths of several horses in the Ukraine were attributed to it.[5] Some even speculate that this type of mold caused the tenth plague addressed in the book of Exodus in the Bible.[6] Black mold gained national attention when it was associated with the deaths of three newborns in Cleveland, Ohio in 1994, and was the reported cause of hemosiderosis, or bleeding lungs, in a number of other newborns, and tests conducted by the Centers for Disease Control and Prevention (CDC) confirmed the presence of elevated levels of black mold in the newborn babies' homes caused by water damage.[7] Later tests associated even more infant deaths that had previously been classified as Sudden Infant Death Syndrome (SIDS) with the black mold.[8] Despite these findings, however, experts have not conclusively linked hemosiderosis to *stachybotrys chartarum* exposure, and continue to study the relationship between *stachybotrys chartarum* and various health problems.[9] The molds "penicillium," "aspergillus," and "alternaria" have also been associated with hypersensitivity, sinusitis, invasive infection, respiratory problems, skin allergies, and pulmonary emphysema, and continue to be studied.[10]

[4] Why Now?

Why has this naturally occurring form of plant life, which exists virtually everywhere and has been around since the beginning of recorded history, gotten such a bad reputation of late? And why have its critics tended to focus on the construction industry?

Part of the answer to these questions lies in heightened public awareness. The information superhighway, that is, the Internet, is littered with mold. A few keystrokes on a computer will now yield hundreds of articles on the hazards of mold and the fortunes they can produce. The accessibility of such information has dramatically increased public awareness and invited litigation. Further compounding this, a number of high-profile celebrities have launched mold litigation and attracted substantial media attention as a result. These include Johnny Carson's former sidekick, Ed McMahon, and Erin Brockovich. Mr. McMahon sued under his homeowner's policy for $20 million alleging that environmental clean-up contractors hired by his insurance company were negligent in failing to properly eliminate water damage caused from a broken pipe.[11] The resulting mold litigation has also produced a number of big-dollar settlements and jury verdicts, which, of course, have only served to encourage even more suits. Some observers theorize that the fact that the average person now spends more time indoors than he/she once did increases the risk of mold-induced health problems.

Changes in the construction industry itself have also made mold-related problems more prevalent. These changes include:

1. "Tighter" building construction:
    a. energy conservation requirements;
    b. the use of exterior wall barriers to reduce or eliminate air infiltration;
2. New building materials and systems:
    a. "EFIS" (Exterior Finish & Insulation Systems, i.e., synthetic stucco);
    b. rain screen building envelope designs;
    c. increased use of cellulosic building materials;

3. HVAC system designs:

    a. reduced and inadequate or improper air flow;

    b. negative air pressure within building;

4. Construction demands/practices:

    a. accelerated fast track construction schedules;

    b. coordination/integration of multiple new products/systems.

[B] Managing the Risk of Mold

In the words of George Jetson: "Hey Jane, how do I stop this crazy thing?!?"

[1] Instant Mold — Just Add Water

To answer that question, let's start by looking at how mold grows. The recipe for making mold is as follows:

1. Take one dose of fungal spores (readily available, for free, everywhere);

2. Place them in favorable temperatures (approximately 50° to 90° Fahrenheit., i.e., virtually any building);

3. Add a food source/nutrients (i.e., organic material — common in most construction materials, dust, and dirt); and

4. Add water (i.e., an adequate moisture supply).

As can be seen from this simple recipe, it is far easier to grow mold than to prevent it. In fact, since it is virtually impossible on most construction projects to prevent the first three ingredients from being present, about the only way to *prevent* mold from growing is to deprive it of moisture.

[2] Water, Water Everywhere — And More Than One Can Drink

The trick, then, is to keep water out. Once water gets in, the trick becomes to get it out. Mold-producing water can enter the construction environment in a variety of ways, including the following:

1. Weather infiltration (note: weather happens);

2. Exposure of construction materials to the elements due to construction schedule and sequencing or ill-conceived material storage techniques;

3. Construction defects;

4. Design defects;

5. Material defects;

6. Improper operation;

7. Improper maintenance;

8. Pipe leaks and breaks;

9. Faulty HVAC and mechanical systems;

10. Leaking windows, doorways, and roofs;

11. Improperly/inadequately sealed roof, wall, and floor penetrations;

12. Penetrable and water permeable curtain walls and exterior wall systems;

13. Flooding;

14. Wicking of subsurface water through building materials; and

15. Other.

To prevent the rampant growth and spread of mold requires controlling humidity and the presence of moisture in the construction environment. To prevent, limit, and control the presence of moisture requires a cooperative and coordinated effort by owners, design professionals, and construction professionals, which includes:

1. A good design.

2. Thorough design review and design quality control (perhaps including a peer review by a separate consultant, focused on mold).

3. Consideration of mold risks in the selection and specification of building materials and methods.

4. Proper training and education of staff.

5. A thorough construction quality control program (including, but not limited to documented inspections).

6. The implementation of all reasonable measures to protect the construction site from the weather.

7. A good program for addressing, determining the root cause/source of, and correcting, water intrusion when it occurs (as it, inevitably, will).

8. Proper project documentation.

9. The implementation of an appropriate insurance program.

10. Good communication and vigilance.

[3] Recognizing and Managing the Risks of Mold

Given the stakes involved, it is imperative that construction industry professionals recognize, address, and proactively manage the risks of mold. Mold is often prevalent in single-family residences, and therefore must be considered and addressed by homeowners and homebuilders. Mold also can appear in a wide array of commercial projects including condominiums, townhouses, hotels, schools, shopping centers, office buildings, governmental buildings, and virtually any structure that will be occupied by human beings.

The Associated General Contractors of America (AGC) recently issued a publication that provides guidance for building owners, construction contractors, and other parties to the construction process for managing the risk of mold in the construction of new buildings. This paper should be on every construction professional's recommended reading list.

In general, some of the steps that should be taken to address the mold issue are as follows:

1. Develop and implement a program for educating and training your workforce.

2. Work with other members of the project team in the planning process to anticipate, address, and avoid the risk of mold.

3. Consider the impact of the construction schedule and sequence on the risk of mold. The important correlation between schedule and sequence and the contractor's exposure to the risk of mold is often overlooked or not understood — generally, the tighter the construction schedule, the greater the risk; contractors should also consider the time of year in which certain construction activities are scheduled to be performed.

4. Consider and address the risk of mold in planning the procurement, delivery, and storage of equipment and materials.

5. Develop and implement a formal mold-prevention program and stated expectations (the same as you would do with safety and other objectives).

6. Address and allocate (using, e.g., appropriate specific warranty, indemnification, and disclaimer language) the risk of mold in the contract.

7. Take all reasonable measures to keep water out (or let it out if it gets in).

8. Ventilate and dehumidify the construction area during construction.

9. Pay careful attention to HVAC and mechanical systems.

10. Be aware and alert, and on the lookout for mold throughout the construction process; implement an early warning system.

11. Document (including photographs) efforts to deliver a mold-free project, and then document that this has been done (perhaps through a "commissioning" program).

12. Make sure to insure against all insurable risks, if it is economically feasible to do so.

13. Do not take or expose employees to any unnecessary risks.

14. Involve the entire project team in resolving any mold-related problems rather than "volunteering" to solve them alone.

15. Designate an individual to be responsible for monitoring the project and protecting the project against the threat of mold.

Mold is now believed to be one potential source of poor indoor air quality (IAQ), and, thus, one potential cause of sick building syndrome (SBS). While the medical community has not yet reached a full consensus regarding the validity, causes, and magnitude of these potential health hazards, it is now clear that, for contractors, the acronyms IAQ and SBS mean at least one thing: SOS, as in *HELP*!

[4] Insurance Ramifications

One of the first questions an owner or a contractor should ask himself or herself in assessing and addressing the risk of mold is: "Do I have insurance for this?" As is often the case in the legal arena, the answer may be unclear. The standard Commercial General Liability (CGL) Policy carried by most contractors contains a number of exclusions that may allow the contractor's insurance carrier to assert that the risk of mold is not covered. These include certain "business risk" exclusions and the "pollution exclusion." The courts that have addressed the issue have reached conflicting conclusions as to whether mold-related claims are covered by a contractor's CGL policy or whether the insurance carrier is relieved of responsibility for such claims under the standard pollution exclusion. Arguments in favor of coverage include: (1) that mold should not be viewed as pollution because it occurs naturally in the environment, and (2) that the language of the exclusion is ambiguous and does not clearly preclude mold coverage.

[5] Specific Mold Exclusions Post 9/11

The national tragedy that rocked the United States on September 11, 2001, has changed our lives in virtually every respect. One change that is particularly relevant to this discussion is that the insurance industry, which took a huge financial hit from 9/11, is: (1) scrutinizing far more closely what risks it is willing to insure, and (2) increasing insurance premiums across the board. These developments, combined with the greatly increased public awareness of the mold problem and the fact that mold claims have now produced a number of multi-million dollar recoveries against insurance companies, have naturally caused many insurance companies to decide to specifically exclude mold claims from the coverage they offer their contractor and owner clients.

Some states have taken steps, either through legislation or by decree of the state insurance commissioner, to prevent insurance companies from excluding mold coverage. While these efforts are well intentioned, the insurance industry has countered by saying that if they are not allowed to exclude mold coverage, they simply will not provide any coverage at all. Whether insurance companies can and will follow through on this threat remains to be seen. There is a distinct possibility, however, that some contractors will not be able to obtain insurance coverage for the risk of mold, or perhaps any insurance coverage at all, either because it is simply unavailable or because the premiums are cost prohibitive.

[C] The Wages of Mold Are Litigation

If appropriate steps are not taken during the design and construction process to prevent mold—and perhaps even if they are—litigation may result. Mold litigation often involves multiple plaintiffs, multiple defendants, multiple claims and cross-claims, multiple theories of recovery, and protracted court proceedings, all of which add up to *a lot of money.*

[1] Round Up the Usual Suspects

Some mold litigation takes the form of class action lawsuits in which literally hundreds of "victims" may join in one lawsuit. The defendants may include owners, developers, contractors, subcontractors, manufacturers, architect/engineers, maintenance contractors, remediation contractors, real estate agents, sellers, landlords, employers, building inspectors, insurance companies and agents, and others — in short, virtually anybody who: (1) may have had something to do with the project, and (2) may have some money.

[2] The Genesis of Mold Claims

As noted previously, the main "active ingredient" in the growth of mold that can potentially be controlled is moisture infiltration. Moisture infiltration can be a product of a sudden event, such as a pipe bursting, or it can be chronic, such as water infiltration through the building exterior via leaks or condensation, or the inability of the building's HVAC system to dehumidify the air.

Problems with an HVAC system were the issue in *Centex-Rooney Construction Co., Inc. v. Martin County,*[12] where employees of a courthouse and office building documented water infiltration through the exterior synthetic hardcoat systems that lead to leaks and to mold growth in the buildings. Upon further investigation, several problems with the buildings' HVAC system were discovered. Specifically, the HVAC system was not in balance: more air was being exhausted than brought in through outdoor air intakes, which created negative pressure, raising the buildings' humidity level. The county brought in several environmental experts who found the presence of two highly unusual and toxigenic molds had created an unhealthy environment and forced the evacuation of the buildings. The relocation, redesign, and reconstruction costs were recouped by the county in the form of an $8,800,000 judgment against the construction company and its sureties.

Some construction and finishing materials are highly susceptible to fungal biodeterioration and infestation. The organic materials contained in gypsum wallboards can be a breeding ground for the toxic mold *stachybotrys chartarum.*[13] Porous insulation, vinyl wall covering, pressed wood

16

products, porous ceiling tiles, and textile wall and floor coverings may also breed toxic mold.[14]

A humid climate can also exacerbate a mold or fungal infiltration through condensation occurring on walls and ceilings when air conditioning cools the surface temperature below the dew point temperature of the contiguous air. For example, in the warm, humid climate of the southeastern United States, warm moisture can easily flow through cracks, openings, and porous materials and allow mold to colonize on the cooler surfaces in the home, such as the wallpaper. A humid environment does not permit wet building materials to dry completely, creating an environment where mold spores flourish and spread. Cases are not, however, limited to the southeast. New York has experienced a sharp increase in mold-related cases with an excess of 400 cases currently pending.[15] In one highly publicized case, 300 tenants in a New York City apartment complex filed a class action suit for $10 billion for mold-related damages.[16] In any climate, a contractor or subcontractor must take extra steps to insure that all porous surfaces are sealed and wet surfaces are allowed to completely dry.

[3] Legal Theories of Liability

[a] Negligence

The primary legal theory under which mold contamination litigation arises is the common law doctrine of negligence.[17] In these cases, the engineer, architect, contractor, subcontractor or developer owes a duty of care to the plaintiff. To determine whether a party has breached his duty of care, the plaintiff must determine the "duty" by examining relevant construction standards. These standards are often not well established and generally come from the testimony of experts, the analysis of building codes, and other relevant evidence. Specifically, many municipal building codes adopt the ventilation requirements and standards established by the American Society of Heating, Refrigeration, and Air-Conditioning Engineers (ASHRAE).[18] The federal government's only direction in this capacity is provided by the United States EPA in "Mold Remediation in Schools and Commercial Buildings."[19] To support a negligence claim, one must establish that the construction professional, engineer, or developer failed to exercise the reasonable degree of care as is ordinarily exhibited by others in the same profession, and as a result, caused the plaintiff(s) to suffer damages. By demonstrating a specialist's failure to abide by the practices of other similarly situated specialists, claims of negligence involving an engineer or an architect are often accompanied by a claim for professional malpractice.

[b] Strict Products Liability

Strict products liability is defined as "liability without fault."[20] Courts apply this theory of liability in cases where the seller, manufacturer, or designer sold any defective or hazardous products expected to reach a consumer that improperly threatens a person's safety. Strict products liability forces the individual or company who manufactured, designed, or supplied the product to pay for any toxic mold damages caused by the defective "product" regardless of whether they deliberately or accidentally caused contamination.[21] Therefore, if a building or HVAC system can be regarded as a defective "product," then the doctrine of strict products liability may apply to the individuals accountable for the building or HVAC system's design, manufacture, and construction if toxic mold is present.[22] In strict liability, the plaintiff is not required to demonstrate the defendant failed to abide by the standard of care of similarly situated engineers, architects, builders, or manufacturers, which is an essential component of a negligence cause of action. Instead, liability may attach to a company or individual who manufactures or designs defective parts that are subsequently incorporated into a building.

A homeowners' association brought an action for strict products liability against a developer and the architects and engineers involved in the construction of an apartment complex in *Del Mar Beach Club Owners Association v. Imperial Contracting Co.*[23] The court in that case held that the developer was liable under a strict products liability theory because the apartment complex was constructed on an unstable bluff. The court held, however, that there was not a reasonable amount of evidence to sustain a cause of action for strict products liability against the engineers or architects because, "those who sell their services for the guidance of others in their economic, financial, and personal affairs are not liable in the absence of negligence or intentional misconduct."

[c] Fraud and Misrepresentation

Claims for fraud and misrepresentation arise from a false statement that is made by a defendant if the defendant knew the statement was false when he/she made it, and intended the plaintiff rely upon it, and if the plaintiff did rely upon it to his/her detriment. For example, a plaintiff may have relied on a defendant's statement that any mold problems present had been corrected when, in fact, such remediation had not been done. An individual may also be liable for fraud if a statement was made to create a false impression on which the plaintiff relied, resulting in damage.

Accordingly, an owner may be liable for fraud and misrepresentation if the owner makes a representation that the structure was inspected and found to be "clean" when such an inspection was never conducted and mold was found to be present. If such a fraudulent statement or false impression causes another party to enter into a contract in reliance on such a statement or impression, the innocent individual may have a right to have the contract rescinded due to the fraudulent inducement to enter into the contract. A claim for fraud and misrepresentation may also be accompanied by a claim for punitive damages if the plaintiff can support that the defendant's behavior was in bad faith.

[d]   Breach of Warranties

In *Greene v. General Motors Corp.*,[24] Mr. Greene sued GM for, among other claims, breach of express and implied warranties, when he alleged that mold present in his Cadillac Escalade caused him to grow colonies of black mold in his sinus cavities and suffer a number of other ailments. The term "warranty" often relates to the quality of a certain product. Purchasers of homes or tenants in a building, or as in the case of Mr. Greene, car purchasers, often take for granted that the structure or the good purchased is safe for its intended use. But what happens when the structure is defective, due to conditions such as an infiltration of toxic mold, which causes the building or good to be unsafe for its intended use? Depending on whether the warranty comes from the language in the contract or the relationship of the parties, an individual may have a breach of warranty claim.

[i] **Express Warranty.** An express warranty is created by statements, facts, or descriptions of goods contained in the contract that were relied upon in execution of the contract. If a clause in a construction contract contains details as to the superior level of quality of the design or the construction of a building, then the provision constitutes an express warranty. Should the building exhibit toxic mold contamination, a plaintiff may successfully argue that the superior level of quality stated in the contract was not achieved, and thus the express warranty contained therein was breached.

[ii] **Implied Warranty.** Where a contractual relationship exists between the parties, but the contract does not contain any express statement as to the quality of the workmanship, a warranty may be implied from the context of the contractual relationship and the reasonable expectations of the parties.[25] As the plaintiff in *Mondelli v. Kendel Homes Corp.*,[26] argued,

19

a party entering into a construction contract has a reasonable expectation that the workmanship will attain a certain minimal standard of workmanship. When toxic mold was found, Mondelli filed an action for breach of the implied warranty of workmanlike quality alleging that the mold infiltration indicates the contractor's failure to meet the minimum standard.

If the infestation of toxic mold is so severe that an owner or renter is unable to live or work in the structure, the individual may have a claim for breach of the implied warranty of habitability. With property rights, comes the right of a certain amount of entitlement to the "quiet enjoyment" of that property. When the continued enjoyment of the building is so severely prohibited by the infestation of toxic mold to make the building uninhabitable, a plaintiff may argue that he was "constructively evicted" from the building; thus, the plaintiff may file a breach of the implied warranty of habitability action.

[e]   *Bad Faith Claims Against Insurance Companies*

If an insurance company is found to have acted in bad faith in relation to the investigation and compensation of a claim related to mold damage, the damages can be substantial. In *Ballard v. Fire Insurance Exchange*,[27] a Texas jury found an insurance company that refused to pay a claim was aware of the toxic mold present in the Ballards' multi-million dollar residence and awarded the family $32 million. The Ballards had filed a claim after experiencing water damage to their custom wood floor that caused it to buckle. The insurance company, which represented the contractor, denied the Ballards' claim and ignored supplemental information regarding the leak and the health problems suffered by members of the family including coughing up blood. While the jury awarded the Ballards $32 million, the punitive damages amount was recently reduced to $28 million by a Texas Appellate Court that held there was insufficient evidence to support the jury's finding of unconscionability on the part of the insurance company.[28] This case is expected to be appealed to the Texas Supreme Court.

[f]   *Personal Injury Claims*

Beyond traditional property damages, a plaintiff may also be awarded damages associated with personal injuries related to mold exposure causing, or worsening, an illness.[29] In *Mazza v. Schurtz*,[30] a California jury awarded the Mazza family $2,700,000 for personal injuries related to exposure of the toxic molds *stachybotrys chartarum*, *penicillium*, and *aspergillus* caused by a leak in a toilet in the residence above the Mazzas.

Another theory of potential liability, "Sick Building Syndrome" or "transient office-related annoyance," has been the subject of many cases where occupants experience a number of symptoms, including burning eyes and headaches, which are associated with time spent in the infected building.[31] These symptoms are often alleviated once the individual has left the building. The source of the problem is often a building's HVAC system spreading mold spores throughout the structure. Accordingly, large numbers of individuals are potentially affected which, in turn, causes the potential damages to increase exponentially. The liable party is then responsible for not only the costs associated with remedying the cause of the mold, but also the medical costs associated with treating the symptoms.

[4]   Damages Recoverable in Mold Cases

The general principle governing the measure of property damages in mold intrusion cases entitles an injured party to recover the reasonable cost of performing reconstruction and repairs in conformance with the original contract's requirements.[32] Accordingly, the cost of mold removal and testing as well as the loss of use and personal property damage may be recovered. These repairs can be costly. The Hilton Hawaiian Village expects to pay $10 million to remove toxic mold from several of its guestrooms.[33] Damages may also include relocation and financing costs as well as engineering and architectural fees reasonably necessary to accomplish reconstruction.[34] In some instances, the infestation of toxic mold may be so severe that the cost of repair is greater than the cost of the property.

In addition to traditional property damages, an individual may recover for pain and suffering, loss of earning capacity, as well as past, present, and future medical bills in a personal injury claim arising from a mold-related sickness.[35]

A defendant may also be held liable for the expenses related to litigation if the defendant is determined to have acted in bad faith.[36] Such bad faith is often established if a plaintiff has informed the defendant of the mold problem and related health issues and such claims have been ignored.

A plaintiff may recover punitive damages in a mold construction defect cause of action if the defendant knew of the hazardous consequences of his poor workmanship and willfully and deliberately chose not to take any precautions to avoid such consequences. In *Anderson v.*

Allstate Insurance Co.,[37] a California jury awarded a 97-year-old plaintiff $18 million in punitive damages after it found the insurance company had maliciously failed to investigate his mold claim associated with a ruptured pipe that flooded the entire interior of his home. The trial judge later reduced the award to a little over $2,700,000, with $500,000 representing damages to the property.

[5]   Possible Defenses

A number of defenses have been successfully asserted against mold claims. A defendant may assert a defense that the statute of limitation has expired, or in other words, the time period for asserting such a claim has elapsed.[38] The applicable statute of limitation would depend on the claim as well as each state's law.

The lack of scientific proof that a plaintiff's injury was a result of the presence of mold may also provide a defense to personal injuries. While some courts have allowed an expert to testify as to the effect mold may have on the health of a plaintiff, the lack of recognized standards may enable a defendant to reduce or eliminate a personal injury claim.[39]

An additional defense may be the plaintiff's failure to mitigate damages. In mold cases, a plaintiff who notices mold must take the necessary steps to limit its growth and cooperate with the defendant to remediate the mold problem.[40] In *Rossmanith v. Union Insurance Co. of Providence,*[41] an insurance company's decision to deny coverage for mold damage was upheld when the court found that the insured failed to alter his home environment once warned about the mold infiltration. If a plaintiff fails to take the recommended steps, the claim may be dismissed.

In cases involving insurance companies, however, the insurance company must establish, as the court in *R.A. Corbett Transport, Inc. v. Oden*[42] held, "not only the [insured's] lack of diligence, but also the amount by which the [insurer's] damages were increased by such failure."

Contributory/comparative negligence may also be a possible defense. If a defendant can show that the plaintiff exacerbated the mold infestation by his own actions, the defendant's contribution to the problem, or significant contribution when compared to the defendant's, may cause the claim to fail.

A precarious balance has been prescribed by the law: while a party must fix, and not exacerbate, the mold infestation, a party must also not destroy evidence of the mold, commonly referred to as "spoliation of the evidence" since a defendant should have an opportunity to examine the infestation of mold before it is destroyed to determine his or the other party's potential liability.

[D] Government to the Rescue

The increase in public concern about mold and mold litigation has not gone unnoticed by legislators at either the state or the federal level. Numerous pieces of legislation have been enacted or proposed throughout the country and many more are sure to follow. As a result, the legal landscape is changing rapidly.

[E] Summary

As the media continues to devote much time and print to the influx of stories related to "toxic mold," the trend toward "mushrooming" mold litigation has become more a probability than a possibility. Scientists and legislatures have begun to answer many of the questions surrounding the effects mold may have on humans. Until those questions are completely answered, however, the mold battle lines will continue to be drawn in the courtroom.

From at least as early as biblical times,[43] mold has been a documented fact of life in our environment. Now, mold litigation is a documented fact of life in the construction industry as well. What was once little more than a nuisance has now been blamed for deaths and illnesses and has become a major risk to the success of a construction project. Prudent construction professionals must recognize and proactively manage these risks.

[1] United States Environmental Protection Agency (EPA), "Mold Remediation in Schools and Commercial Buildings," Publication EPA 402-K-01-001, March 2001.

[2] Thor Kamban Biberman, "Dormitory at San Diego State Closed over Toxic Mold," San Diego Daily, July 2, 2001, p.1B.

[3] Dolnick, David, "'Toxic' Mold Part I: What Is It? What Causes It? And Why Do We Keep Hearing About It?!," Constructor Magazine, Oct. 2001.

[4] Nelson, Berlin D., Ph.D. "*Stachybotrys Chartarum*: The Toxic Indoor Mold," Am. Phytopathological Soc'y, Feature Story, Nov. 2001.

[5] Mahmoudi, M. Gershwin, "Sick Building Syndrome. III. *Stachybotrys Chartarum*," J. of Asthma, Vol. 34, No. 2, pp. 191–198.

[6] Marr, JS, "Letter: Effects of Mycotoxins in Health and Disease," JAMA, Vol. 78, No. 13, p. 1062 (1997).

[7] Centers for Disease Control & Prevention. "Acute Pulmonary Hemorrhage/Hemosiderosis Among Infants — Cleveland, January 1993-November 1994," Morbidity and Mortality Rep., Vol. 43, No. 48, Dec. 9, 1994, available at <http://www.cdc.gov/cdc.htm>.

[8] Centers for Disease Control & Prevention, "Update on Pulmonary Hemorrhage/Hemosiderosis Among Infants-Cleveland, Ohio, 1993–1996," Morbidity and

Mortality Weekly Rep., Vol. 46, No. 2, Jan. 17, 1997, available at
<http://www.cdc.gov/cdc.htm>.

[9] Centers for Disease Control & Prevention, "Update: Pulmonary
Hemorrhage/Hemosiderosis Among Infants—Cleveland, Ohio, 1993–1996," Morbidity
and Mortality Weekly Rep., Vol. 49, No. 9, March 10, 2000.

[10] Cohen, Sylvie, M.D., et al., "Molds," Geo. Wash. Univ. Center, Washington, D.C.,
2002.

[11] O'Neill, Ann, "Ed McMahon Sues over Mold in House," Los Angeles Times, April
10, 2002, p. 1.

[12] 706 So. 2d 20 (Fla. Dist. Ct. App. 1998).

[13] Andersen, et al., "Characterization of *Stachybotrys* from Water-Damaged Buildings
Based on Morphology, Growth, and Metabolite Production," Mycologia, Vol. 94, No. 3
(2002).

[14] Air Quality Sciences, Inc., "AirfAQS Extra," Laboratory Services Update, Vol. 8,
No. 4 (2002).

[15] General Cologne, "RE: Hazardous Times Burgeoning Mold Claims," Feb. 2002
Issue, <www.grc.com>.

[16] Herndon, EL, Jr. & Yang, CS, "Mold and Mildew: A Creeping Catastrophe,"
Mealey's Mold Litigation Conference Materials, p. 333 (June 2001).

[17] *Sabella v. Wisler*, 377 P.2d 889 (Cal.1963).

[18] Del. Code Ann. tit. 16, § 7602 (2002).

[19] Available at <http://www.epa.gov/iaq/molds/index.html>.

[20] Black's Law Dictionary 815 (6th ed. 1990).

[21] *Del Mar Beach Club Owners Ass'n v. Imperial Contracting Co.*, 176 Cal. Rptr. 886,
888 (Ct. App. 1981).

[22] *Blackhawk Corp. v. Gotham Ins. Co.*, 54 Cal. App.4th 1090 (1997).

[23] 176 Cal. Rptr. 886, 889 (Ct. App. 1981).

[24] No. 02CV156 (N.C. Super., Wataugo Co.).

[25] *Pollard v. Saxes & Yolles*, 12 Cal. 3d 374, 377 (1974).

[26] 631 N.W.2d 846 (Neb. 2001).

[27] No. 99-05252 (250th District Ct., Travis Co., Tx.).

[28] Robbins, Mary Alice, "Punitives in Mold Case Slashed by $28 Million," Miami
Daily Business Review, Vol. 77, No. 143 (Jan. 2, 2003).

[29] *Mazza v. Schurtz*, No. 00AS04795 (Super. Ct., Sacramento Co., Cal., Nov. 7, 2001).

[30] *Id.*

[31] Seider, A., "Sick Building Syndrome," Hospital Practice, Vol. 34, No. 4, pp.
127–129 (1999).

[32] *Ghadir Ayaz, et al. v. Fullmer Constr.*, No. 00CC06647 (Calif. Super. Ct., 2002).

[33] "Mold Forces Hilton Hawaii to Shut Down 453 Rooms," N.Y. Times, Aug. 9, 2002.

[34] *Centex-Rooney Constr. Co., Inc. v. Martin County*, 706 So. 2d 20 (Fla. Dist. Ct.
App. 1998).

[35] *Katayama Int'l & Mayatek Corp. v. Republic W. Ins. Co.*, No. 98A500946 (Calif.
Super. Ct., 2002).

[36] *Daniel Hatley, et al. v. Century Nat'l Ins. Co.*, No. CV2000-006713 (Ariz. Super.
Ct. 2002).

[37] 2000 U.S. Dist. LEXIS 20847 (E.D. Cal. 2000), *on appeal*, 45 Fed. Appx. 754
(2002).

[38] *Searle v. City of Rochelle*, 293 A.D.2d 735 (N.Y. 2d Dept. 2002).

[39] Goldman, Steven, "Toxic Mold is Here to Stay," N.Y.L.J., April 3, 2002.

[40] *Allison v. W. Del Amo Pac. Condo Assoc.*, No. YC040331 (Calif. Super. Ct. 2002).

[41] 2001 WL 1451050 (Iowa App., Nov. 16, 2001).

[42] 678 S.W.2d 172 (Tex. Ct. App. 1984).

[43] Leviticus 14:44–45.

CHAPTER 7

TITLE INSURANCE IN COMMERCIAL REAL ESTATE TRANSACTIONS

John C. Murray

§ 7.05   COVERED RISKS: THE INSURING PROVISIONS

Page 381, add to note 6:

The ALTA title policy coverage for "unmarketability of title" pertains only to those unmarketability claims resulting from title defects; unmarketability problems relating to the use of the property are not ordinarily covered by the title policy. For example, off-record environmental contamination is not a risk covered by the insuring provisions of the standard title insurance policy. Such contamination is not a "defect, lien or encumbrance," and is not a matter affecting marketability of title.

There need not be an "adverse claimant" in order to raise an unmarketability claim. The mere possibility of a "cloud" on title, sufficient to justify a potential buyer or lender in declining to buy or lend on the property, is enough to trigger coverage under the policy.

Unmarketability of title is not necessarily the same as reduction in market value. The insured may suffer a loss, when selling or mortgaging a property as a result of a title defect that was not discovered or disclosed in the original title search, that cannot be adequately measured by (as stated in the owner's policy for calculation of loss) "the difference between the value of the insured estate or interest as insured and the value of the insured estate or interest subject to the defect." If the buyer refuses to purchase the property because the seller is unable to deliver title in the condition specified in the purchase agreement, the loss to the insured triggered by the sale of the property may be different from a loss otherwise incurred by the insured after the closing.

"Perfect title" may be defined as title "without fault, defect or omission." Providing coverage against loss by reason of unmarketability of title is different from that of certifying that the owner or the mortgagor "in fact" or "in law" is possessed of a marketable title. *See, e.g., Crown Enters., Inc. v. Trustco Bank N.A.*, 2001 N.Y. Slip Op. 400779U, 2001 N.Y. Misc. LEXIS 452 (Sup. Ct. of N.Y., Rensselaer Co., July 16, 2001) ("a title company's unconditional approval to insure a particular title does not necessarily render that title marketable," citing 12 Warren's Weed New York Real Property, 4th ed. (Matthew Bender)).

Essentially, title is "umarketable" if an "alleged" or "apparent" matter would permit a purchaser who has contracted to buy the real estate to cancel on grounds of unmarketability. Exactly what constitutes a marketable title is a matter of judicial interpretation. State courts have varying definitions of this term. For example, courts have defined marketable title as "free from reasonable doubt," "free from defects and encumbrances," "title a reasonable [or prudent] person would accept," "not a perfect title but one which is not subject to reasonable doubt nor does it require litigation," "title that may be freely made the subject of resale and that can be sold at a fair price to a reasonable purchaser or mortgaged to a person of reasonable prudence as security for the loan of money," "one that is relatively free from doubt, such that in a suit for specific performance a court would compel the prospective purchaser to accept title," and title that is "free from reasonable doubt and such as reasonably well informed and intelligent purchasers, exercising ordinary business caution, would be willing to accept." However, at least one case, *Stewart Title Guaranty Co. v. Greenlands Realty, L.L.C.*, 58 F. Supp. 2d 360 (D.N.J. 1999), has held that title is not rendered unmarketable by an alleged defect that is not reasonably debatable or by the threat of litigation that has "no reasonable justification."

In *Mellinger v. TICOR Title Ins. Co.*, 13 Cal. Rptr. 357 (Ct. App. 2001), the court stated: "Based on the meaning of marketable title established by the Supreme Court, the question is whether a reasonable purchaser, knowing that a third party might claim an interest in the property, would nonetheless proceed with the transaction." The court held that whether an encroachment was evidenced in the real property records was a question of fact for the jury, and it refused to concur with an Illinois decision that treated the issue as a question of law. (The court acknowledged that the policy's survey exception might later be found to be applicable to exclude coverage, but stated that it was first appropriate to decide whether coverage existed in the first place under the terms of the policy).

In a loan policy, this insuring proviso ("Unmarketability of the Title") covers the lender against title-related claims that actually disable or prevent the lender from selling his or her (or its) mortgage to another investor, or would require the lender to repurchase a mortgage. As noted above, this language does not cover circumstances resulting from physical condition of the land, such as contamination with hazardous waste or damage to improvements.

Although the ALTA title policy forms define the term "public records" (in Section 1(f) of the Conditions and Stipulations), the policy does not limit its coverage to matters of record title only. However, it does limit the title company's obligation for searching to the public records as defined in the policy.

What if the defect is not of record, but could have been identified if a survey had been done and submitted to the title insurer? Since the policy does not limit coverage to record matters, the title insurer must either take a general survey exception, or examine the survey and take specific exception to the items shown on the survey. If the title insurer takes specific exceptions for items shown on the survey, but misses a matter that should have been excepted and does not show it as a specific exception (such as an encroachment), the title insurer should be liable if the buyer repudiates the contract and refuses to close because it has discovered the defect and refuses to close the transaction.

§ 7.07   CREDITORS' RIGHTS

Page 391, add at end of first full paragraph:

Section 101(54) of the Bankruptcy Code (Code) defines "transfer" as "every mode, direct or indirect, absolute or conditional, voluntary or involuntary, of disposing of or parting with property or with an interest in property, including retention of title as a security interest and foreclosure of the debtor's equity of redemption." Under § 548(d)(1) of the Code, the date of transfer, for fraudulent conveyance purposes, is the date on which the transfer would have become perfected against a subsequent bona fide purchaser under applicable state law. A debtor may make a "transfer" by, among other things, incurring a debt or obligation or providing a guaranty, making a payment, granting a lien or security interest on its assets, or transferring all or a portion of its property. To constitute a fraudulent transfer under § 548(a)(1) of the Code, the transfer must be made with actual intent to hinder, delay, or defraud a creditor. Actual intent to defraud need not be shown by direct evidence, but may be inferred from the circumstances surrounding the conveyance, including reckless disregard of the consequences of the transaction and the subsequent conduct of the parties.

Page 392, add at end of first full paragraph:

The UFTA distinguishes between present and future creditors, and specifies the types of transfers that are fraudulent in each case. A transfer made or an obligation incurred is fraudulent as to present *and* future creditors if the debtor-transferor made the transfer or incurred the obligation "with actual intent to hinder, delay or defraud any creditor." UFTA § 4 (b). Section 4(b) lists 11 factors to be considered in determining actual intent to defraud creditors. Under the UFCA, creditors can avoid conveyances made and obligations incurred by a person "with actual intent, as distinguished from intent presumed in law, to hinder, delay or defraud either present or future creditors." It is clear, under each of these statutory schemes (as well as under § 548 of the Code), that both present *and* future creditors have the ability to avoid intentionally fraudulent transfers. As noted earlier, the bankruptcy trustee or DIP can avoid any transfer made or obligation incurred with intent to "hinder, delay or defraud" any creditor. Each of these "badges of fraud" is stated in the disjunctive; therefore, a creditor need only show one type of intent in order to succeed in proving that the transfer is "intentionally" fraudulent.

Both present and future creditors may recover under the UFTA when a transfer occurs for less than reasonably equivalent value and the transfer results in the debtor's capital being unreasonably small in relation to the business or transaction in which the debtor is, or is about to be, engaged, and when the transfer is made without receiving reasonably equivalent value and the debtor intends to incur debts beyond the ability to pay. Present creditors (but not future creditors) may recover property under the UFTA when it is transferred by the debtor for less than reasonably equivalent value if the debtor is insolvent or is rendered insolvent by the transfer, or when the transfer is to an insider without receiving reasonably equivalent value when the debtor is insolvent.

Page 393, add at note 15:

See also Federal Nat'l Mortgage Ass'n v. Fitzgerald (In re Fitzgerald) (Fitzgerald II), 255 B.R. 807, 810 (Bankr. D. Conn. 2000) (reaffirming court's rationale in *In re Fitzgerald, supra*, and finding that Connecticut made legislative decision "not to accord a conclusive presumption of 'reasonably equivalent value' to strict foreclosures under state fraudulent transfer law"). *But see Talbot v. Federal Home Loan Mortgage Corp (In re Talbot)*, 254 B.R. 63, 68–70 (Bankr. D. Conn. 2000) (holding that judgment entered under Connecticut's strict foreclosure law conclusively established that "reasonably equivalent value" was received and precluded debtors from asserting that foreclosure judgment was constructively fraudulent transfer).

Page 393, add to note 16:

But see In re Grandote Country Club Co., Ltd., 252 F.3d 1146, 1152 (10th Cir. 2001) (transfer of real property was for reasonably equivalent value, and not fraudulent under Colorado Uniform Fraudulent Transfer Act, where defendant acquired property through regularly conducted tax sale under Colorado law subject to competitive bidding procedure); *In re Samaniego*, 224 B.R. 154 (Bankr. E.D. Wash. 1998); *Russell-Polk v. Bradley (In re Russell-Polk)*, 200 B.R. 218 (Bankr. E.D. Mo. 1996) (same); *Hollar v. Myers (In re Hollar)*, 184 B.R. 243 (Bankr. M.D.N.C. 1995) (same); *Lord v. Neumann (In re Lord)*, 179 B.R. 429 (Bankr. E.D. Pa. 1995) (same).

Page 394, add at end of first full paragraph:

The types of conduct found by bankruptcy courts to have justified equitable subordination include (1) an "insider" creditor who, despite having full knowledge that the debtor was undercapitalized and insolvent, advanced funds to the debtor in the form of loans when no other third-party lender would have done so; (2) a creditor engaged in conduct that was tantamount to overreaching; (3) a lender's agent misrepresented the availability of construction and take-out financing; (4) a secured creditor misrepresented the debtor's ability to pay trade creditors (resulting in the subordination of the secured claim to the unsecured claims of a trade creditor); and (5) a lender controlled the debtor's plant and cash disbursements and had received a voidable preference.

The bankruptcy court generally invokes these sanctions when the lender has engaged in overreaching or lender control, which occurs when the lender steps beyond the traditional role of a lender and participates in the debtor's business or engages in other egregious conduct that justifies the use of the court's equitable powers. As mentioned above, in these situations the court may decide to subordinate, recharacterize, or even disallow a transaction. In general, the equitable subordination doctrine is limited to reordering priorities, and does not permit total disallowance of a claim. However, if the conduct of the creditor is so egregious that it affect the validity of the claim under applicable principles of law, the debtor can ask the court to disallow it in full as part of the claims avoidance process.

Page 395, add at end of last paragraph:

For example, in *In re Dorholt*, 239 B.R. 521 (B.A.P. 8th Cir. 2000), the court held that a security interest perfected 16 days after value was advanced due to mistake by a service bureau was a substantially contemporaneous transfer, precluding avoidance of the lien as a preferential transfer.

§ 7.09   COMMERCIAL ENDORSEMENT COVERAGES

[E]   Special Risk Endorsements

[3]   Recharacterization

[c]   *Mezzanine Financing*

Page 433, add at end of subsection:

The borrower in a mezzanine loan is often a limited liability company (LLC), and the equity participant in the borrowing entity is frequently itself an LLC. In those situations where the mezzanine lender is taking a pledge of some or all of the equity interests in one or more of these entities in connection with the mezzanine loan, the lender may look to the title insurer for special forms of title-insurance coverage. The lender may seek some form of non-imputation coverage, *i.e.*, an endorsement offering assurance that the title insurer will not deny coverage under the owner's policy based on matters known to the borrowing entity (or its members) being imputed to the lender.

Title underwriters may require an affidavit and an indemnity agreement from the existing LLC members, and from the mezzanine lender when it exercises its foreclosure rights under the pledge and succeeds to an ownership interest in the mezzanine borrower. These affidavits and indemnity agreements will state that the respective parties have no knowledge of any fact that will affect the coverage under the policy, and will hold the title insurer harmless for losses resulting from its reliance on such affidavits and indemnities. The title insurer may also require, and review, financial statements from all relevant parties in order to achieve a comfort level for relying on the aforementioned indemnity.

Mezzanine-financing endorsements customarily offered by title insurers state that (as agreed to by the insured and its equity members) all payments for loss under the policy will go directly to the mezzanine lender, and that there will be no denial of coverage as the result of the transfer of any of the LLC membership interests to the mezzanine lender. The endorsements further provide that the title insurer waives its right of subrogation and indemnity against any of the insured owner's equity owners until the mezzanine loan is paid in full. If a loss occurs under the policy, the amount paid by the title insurer is limited to the actual loss less a percentage thereof equal to the percentage of LLC membership interests not owned by the mezzanine lender at such time. If the loss occurs before the mezzanine lender's acquisition of the insured owner's membership interests, the mezzanine lender is not required first to pursue its remedies against other collateral. However, the title insurer's liability in any event is limited to the amount of the mezzanine loan, and the title insurer is entitled to credit for any amount paid out under a simultaneous loan policy. The title insurer is also entitled to reimbursement from payments received by the mezzanine lender from other security. The term "mezzanine lender" can be defined to include the owner of the mezzanine loan and each successor in interest in ownership of the mezzanine loan, and include any subsidiary or affiliate entity of the owner of the mezzanine loan. The availability and content of the endorsements will vary depending on factual and underwriting considerations, as well as statutory and regulatory restraints in certain states.

Mezzanine financing often involves extending credit to equity holders of an LLC, with the lender taking a pledge of the parties' equity interests in the LLC. Under § 9-102(a)(49) of Revised Article 9 (Revised Article 9) of the Uniform Commercial Code (UCC) (which was enacted into law in all 50 states in 2001), these types of assets can be either "investment property" or "general intangibles." Investment property is defined, under § 9-102(a)(49), as a security (whether certificated or uncertificated), security entitlement, securities account, and commodity account or commodity contract. A security interest in investment property may be perfected by control, by filing, or, if the investment property is a certificated security, by possession. *See* UCC §§ 8-301, and §§ 9-313(a) and 9-328 of Revised Article 9. Under § 9-102 (a)(42) of Revised Article 9, general intangibles are defined as personal property, including things in action, other than accounts, chattel paper, commercial tort claims, deposit accounts, documents, goods, instruments, investment property, letter-of-credit rights, letters of credit, money, and oil, gas, or other minerals before extraction. The term includes a "payment intangible" (defined in

§ 9-102(a)(61) of Revised Article 9 as "a general intangible under which the account debtor's principal obligation is a monetary obligation") and software. In essence, "general intangibles" is the residual category of personal property that is not included in the other defined types of collateral. A security interest in a general intangible is perfected by filing. *See* § 9-310 of Revised Article 9.

In order to have a priority security interest in the pledged collateral that will prevail over purchasers, other lenders, and creditors using judicial process to obtain a lien on the collateral, the mezzanine lender must perfect its interest in the collateral. *See* § 9-308(a) of Revised Article 9. As stated above, perfection of a security interest in a pledge of an interest in an LLC can be accomplished by (1) filing a UCC-1 financing statement in the appropriate jurisdiction (under § 9-310 of Revised Article 9, if the security interest is deemed a general intangible or is investment property); (2) taking possession of the collateral (under § 9-313(a) of Revised Article 9, which also provides that a perfected security interest in certificated securities may be obtained by taking delivery of the certificated securities under UCC § 8-301); or (3) control (under § 9-314(c) of Revised Article 9, if the security interest is deemed investment property). While the general rule is that the earlier of the first to file or perfect has established priority, perfection by control will prime a security interest in the same property that is perfected by any other method of perfection, even if the control occurs after the time of first perfection. *See* § 9-328(1) of Revised Article 9. Section 9-331(b) of Revised Article 9 also makes explicit what was implied under former Article 9 and is explicit under Article 8, *i.e.*, where investment property collateral is transferred to a person protected under UCC Article 8, Article 9 defers to the rights of protected purchasers under Article 8, to the extent Article 8 provides rights to those protected persons. *See* § 9-331 of Revised Article 9. Thus, although perfection by filing is available, to the extent possible lenders should always seek to perfect their interests in pledges of LLC membership interests by control.

If the governing documents of an LLC provide that the membership interests are securities, then such interests will be treated as securities instead of general intangibles. If an issuer thus opts into Article 8, the lender's interest in the collateral is deemed investment property and the lender can obtain "Protected Purchaser Status" under UCC § 8-303. A lender has "Protected Purchaser Status" when it gives value for the interest without notice of any adverse claim and has control of the security. Protected Purchaser Status will enable the lender to defeat any adverse claim, including claims of third parties that treat their interests as general intangibles and who perfect by filing in the jurisdiction in which the debtor is located.

The issuer's counsel should be cognizant of the effect of opting into Article 8 and be careful to follow the mandates required within Article 8. For example: (1) § 8-202 requires the issuer to set forth the terms of the security on the certificate or to incorporate them by reference; (2) § 8-204 requires the issuer to conspicuously note restrictions on transfer on the security certificate or, if uncertificated, to notify the registered owner; (3) § 8-205 provides, under certain circumstances, for the effectiveness of unauthorized signatures; (4) § 8209 provides that a lien in favor of an issuer is effective against a purchaser only if the right of the issuer to the lien is noted conspicuously on the security certificate; (5) § 8401 sets forth the requirements under which an issuer shall register a requested transfer of a certificated or uncertificated security; and (6) § 8404 provides criteria for holding the issuer liable for wrongful registration.

Section 9-106 of Revised Article 9, by reference to UCC § 8-106, provides that a secured party takes control of an uncertificated security, such as a pledge of an uncertificated LLC membership interest, "if either it is delivered to the purchaser or the issuer agrees in a written agreement to follow the written instructions of the purchaser without further consent by the registered owner." Delivery will occur, under UCC § 8-103, when the issuer registers the purchaser (*i.e.*, the lender), or a third party not closely related to or controlled by the debtor — other than a securities intermediary — who holds on behalf of the lender, as the registered owner.

Control of a certificated security occurs when the lender or a third person not closely connected to or controlled by the debtor has possession of the certificate, and when the certificate is (1) issued in bearer form, (2) issued to the debtor as owner with an endorsement in blank, or (3) the lender has an assignment separate from the certificate signed in blank by the debtor. *See* § 9-106 of Revised Article 9 and UCC § 8-106. *See also* Steven O. Weise, Philip Ebeling, Dena M. Cruz, Theodore H. Sprink, and Randall L. Scott, *It's Time to Take a Close Look at UCC Article* 9, 19 Cal. Real Prop. J. 3, 7–8 (2001).

According to one commentator:

> A lender requiring an opt-in should take steps to prevent the issuer from opting out of Article 8 at a later time [by entering into in an agreement with the issuer that it will not opt out and requiring that the LLC oper-ating agreement provide that the language opting in to Article 8 cannot be amended without the lender's consent]. A lender that does not require an opt-in should take steps to prevent an opt-in [by entering into

an agreement with the issuer that it will not opt in under Article 8 or amend the LLC operating agreement to permit an opt-in without the lender's consent].

Lynn A. Soukup, *"Opting In" to Article 8—LLC, GP & LP Interests as Collateral,* Commercial Law Newsletter, American Bar Association Section of Business Law (July 2002), at p. 1.

First American Title Insurance Company, Fidelity Title Insurance Company, and Stewart Title Insurance Corporation now issue UCC title insurance policies. The basic policies offered by these companies insure the proper creation, attachment, perfection *by filing* (taking exception for interests perfected by possession or control), priority and effectiveness of UCC security interests. In connection with this UCC title policy, First American has also promulgated a specialized endorsement for use in connection with mezzanine loans that insures perfection by possession and control. Remarkably, if the governing documents of an LLC provide that the membership interests are securities and the lender has taken the proper steps to achieve Protected Purchaser status (as described above), this endorsement also insures that the pledgor owns the interests being pledged as collateral.

Page 453, add new subsection at end of page:

[F]   Leasehold Policy

On October 13, 2001, the American Land Title Association (ALTA) adopted the new ALTA 13 Leasehold Owner's Endorsement and ALTA 13.1 Leasehold Loan Endorsement (hereinafter collectively referred to as "2001 Leasehold Endorsements"). With the adoption of these endorsements, the old owner's and lender's leasehold policies are withdrawn (although they may still be available to those who wish to use them until they get comfortable with the new endorsements). These new forms may be obtained by accessing the ALTA Web site (*alta.org*), and clicking on the link that says "New Forms Proposed by the ALTA Forms Committee." The new endorsements were created to address and, one would hope, alleviate the concerns of various title insurance customer groups, who believed that the coverage under existing forms of leasehold policies did not adequately address the current realities of leasehold ownership and financing. The new endorsements provide significantly expanded coverage, as well as much needed clarification of essential terms. (Copies of the 2001 Leasehold Owner's Endorsement and 2001 Leasehold Loan

Endorsement are attached hereto as Exhibit "A" and Exhibit "B," respectively. All terms hereinafter capitalized are capitalized terms in the 2001 Leasehold Endorsements).

The ALTA adopted standard owner's and lender's leasehold policy forms in 1975 (hereinafter collectively referred to as "1975 Leasehold Policies"). The format of the 1975 Leasehold Policies is similar in most respects to the standard owner's and lender's policy forms. The insured under a leasehold policy is generally concerned about the same risks that exist in connection with basic owner's and lender's policies, including the following: the true nature of the landlord entity; the conditions, covenants, and restrictions that might affect the operation and use of the leased property; outstanding encumbrances such as mortgages and deeds of trust (and assurance of rights granted by recorded non-disturbance agreements) that might affect the tenant's right of possession; the existence of third-party rights such as options to purchase and rights of first refusal; expansion rights granted to other tenants; and the tenant's right of uninterrupted possession of the property for the entire lease term (including renewals).

The 1975 Leasehold Policies define the insured "leasehold estate" as "the right of possession for the term or terms described in Schedule A hereof subject to any provisions contained in the Lease which might limit the right of possession." This limits the title company's obligation solely to the tenant's possessory rights in the property, and does not include other landlord obligations such as maintenance, repair, or the obligation to supply utilities to the premises.

For the purpose of determining a loss under the 1975 Leasehold Policies, the value of the leasehold estate "shall consist of the then present worth of the excess, if any, of the fair market rental value of the estate or interest, undiminished by any matters for which claim is made, for that part of the term stated in Schedule A then remaining plus any renewal or extended term for which a valid option to renew or extend is contained in the Lease, over the value of the rent and other consideration required to be paid under the Lease for the same period."

This method of valuation is customarily based on an appraisal as of the time of loss, based on the difference between the fair market value of the leased property and the value of the rent required to be paid for the remainder of the lease term. If the tenant has a favorable below-market lease rental it will recover the additional cost required to lease new space; otherwise, it will not recover under this method of determining value. The 1975 Leasehold Policies also provide additional coverage and damages for the following items of loss: the reasonable cost of removing and relocating personal property, including transportation for the initial 25 miles, and the reasonable cost of repairing any personal property damaged during such removal and relocation (note that most leasehold improvements would not be covered under this item of loss because "personal property" is defined as chattels that can be removed without appreciable damage to the property; the determination of whether a particular item is a fixture or personal property likely will be based on applicable state statutory and case law); any rent or damages that the owner of the leasehold estate may be obligated to pay, prior to eviction, to any party determined to have a paramount title to that of the lessor in the lease; the amount of rent that the owner of the leasehold estate may be required to pay to the lessor after it has been evicted from the land; the fair market value of any sublease entered into by the owner of the leasehold estate existing at the date of eviction; and any damages that the owner of the leasehold estate is obligated to pay to any sublessee on account of breach of the sublease caused by eviction of the insured.

The problem with the 1975 Leasehold Policies, at least as perceived more than a quarter-century later by title insurance customer groups, is that these policies were designed to provide basic protection primarily for a tenant leasing space in an office building where the cost of tenant improvements is insignificant and the tenant's business does not depend on being in a specific location. These customer groups argued that the coverage provided by the 1975 Leasehold Policies does not protect major tenants (such as large law firms) who may have hundreds of thousands (or even millions) of dollars invested in tenant improvements and who are forced to vacate the leased premises because of failure of the lessor's title or the foreclosure of a prior lien. They further argued that the 1975 Leasehold Owner's Policy does not protect the purchaser of a business or one or more retail facilities (such as a chain of fast-food restaurants), who considers the unique location of such property or properties and the goodwill generated thereby as important items of valuation when deciding to purchase the leasehold interest(s).

Another perceived shortcoming with the 1975 Leasehold Policies was the failure to address the needs of purchasers of ground leasehold estates, where the tenant anticipates constructing and financing significant leasehold improvements. Since the determination of loss under these policies does not take into account the value of these improvements, ground lessees and their lenders instead would often ask for the standard ALTA owner's and lender's policies, which would insure the tenant's (or lender's) leasehold interest in the property and a fee interest or estate for years in the leasehold improvements constructed by the tenant. These policies also would contain an exception for the ground lessor's fee interest, and would include an endorsement providing that any loss under the policy would be calculated so as to include all loss of value to the insured of its interest as owner of the improvements located on the land. The reason for this endorsement was to obtain the benefit of the revised method of determination of loss stated therein, instead of the limited loss coverage provided by the 1975 Leasehold Policies. *See* Harvey L. Temkin, *Reformulating the ALTA Leasehold Title Insurance Policy*, The ACREL Papers: Fall 2000, at Tab 18.

The 2001 Leasehold Endorsements provide significantly improved and enhanced coverage for leasehold owners and lenders, and effectively deal with each of the customer concerns described above. These endorsements are designed primarily for long-term commercial leases with significant tenant improvements, and will be attached either to an owner's (or lender's) policy that covers a leasehold estate alone or that covers a leasehold estate in the land and the ownership interests in the improvements to be constructed or paid for by the insured tenant. The existing Leasehold Conversion Endorsement will be retained for residential leasehold transactions.

The definition of "Lease Term," as set forth in Section 1.g. of the 2001 Leasehold Endorsements, has been modified for clarity; it refers to "the duration of the Leasehold estate, including any renewal or extended term, if a valid option to renew or extend is contained in the Lease." (Note: this definition would not cover lease extensions or rights granted after the effective date of the title policy, in the absence of the issuance of a new endorsement covering such rights). Also, the definition of "Leasehold Estate," as set forth in Section 1.c. of the 2001 Leasehold Endorsements, is limited to "the right of possession for the Lease Term," and has deleted the (often contentious) language in the 1975 Leasehold Policy Forms that made the coverage subject to lease provisions that limited the tenant's right of possession. The ALTA Forms Committee also decided not to raise a specific Schedule B exception for duties and obligations of the tenant under the lease. The ALTA Forms Committee reasoned that no specific Schedule B exception was necessary because of Exclusion 3(a) of the ALTA Owner's and Loan Policies, which excludes from coverage those matters "created, suffered, assumed or agreed to by the insured claimant."

Section 1.g. of the 2001 Leasehold Endorsements defines "Tenant Leasehold Improvements" as "improvements, including landscaping, required or permitted to be built on the land by the Lease that have been built at the insured's expense or in which the insured has an interest greater than the right to possession during the Lease Term." This language is modified from that contained in the 1975 Leasehold Policies, to make it clear that the tenant's interest in the improvements will only be covered if the tenant has paid for the improvements or has more than a possessory right therein; otherwise the tenant's rights in the property would be adequately covered under the definition of "Leasehold Estate." Because of the desire of tenants who construct substantial improvements to obtain the benefits of tax depreciation thereon, it is likely that the tenant will seek to be characterized as the owner of the improvements during the term of the lease. A leasehold-mortgage lender should make certain that this is so in order to obtain the full benefit of the extended coverage provided under the new leasehold lender's endorsement. As noted above, the endorsement provides that the lender will be covered for the value of the improvements upon foreclosure only if it has a right greater than possession or has paid for the improvements. Therefore, the lender should make certain that the tenant's ownership of the improvements is clearly documented, or, if the lender's loan is financing non-owned improvements, it should clearly document the use of the loan funds for construction of the improvements.

Section 2 of the 2001 Leasehold Owner's Endorsement now states that "subsection (b) of Section 7 of the Conditions and Stipulations shall not apply to any Leasehold Estate covered by this policy." This is in reference to the "coinsurance" provision of the standard ALTA Owner's policy (coinsurance does not apply with respect to the loan policy), which reduces the amount of coverage available to the insured if an insufficient amount of insurance is obtained for the property (thus disincentivizing an insured from attempting to obtain inexpensive "defense cost" insurance). Because it is often difficult to accurately value a leasehold estate alone (as opposed to the leasehold estate with improvements) and most leasehold purchasers do not wish initially to incur the expense of an appraisal, the ALTA Forms Committee decided not to impose the coinsurance requirement. However, this exemption from the coinsurance requirement applies only to the valuation of the Leasehold Estate, and does not apply to the valuation of Tenant Leasehold Improvements, which present fewer valuation problems (because a construction budget usually has been prepared showing the cost of constructing the improvements) and is closer to the type of situation that the coinsurance provision was meant to cover.

The purchaser of a leasehold estate should be careful to estimate as closely as possible the amount of coverage for both the leasehold and tenant-improvement components, because the loss coverage in any event will be limited to the amount of insurance stated in Schedule A of the policy. The 2001 Leasehold Endorsements have substantially revised the definition of "Valuation of Estate or Interest Insured." Section 3 of the 2001 Leasehold Owners' Endorsement (Section 2 in the 2001 Leasehold

Loan Endorsement) states that the value of the insured's estates or inter-ests "shall consist of the value for the Remaining Lease Term of the Leasehold Estate and any Tenant Leasehold Improvements existing on the date of the Eviction. The insured claimant shall have the right to have the Leasehold Estate and the Tenant Improvements valued as a whole or separately." This new provision allows for a negotiated basis for valuation of both the Leasehold Estate and the Tenant Leasehold Improvements if they are to be valued separately. If a subsequent loss occurs, the "value" of the leasehold interest for the Remaining Lease Term will be determined by appraisal, which may consist, at the option of the insured, either of a calculation of the value of both the Leasehold Estate and the Tenant Leasehold Improvements, or a separate calculation of the value of each of these components. The insured will be able to offer as proof of loss what-ever damages it claims it has incurred by virtue of its loss of possession, and will not be limited by the language in the 1975 Leasehold Policies that restricted coverage to the difference between the fair market rental value of the leased premises for the remainder of the lease term and the value of the rent required to be paid under the lease for the same period.

This new method of valuation of leasehold interests constitutes a substantial expansion of coverage available to the insured and may obvi-ate the need for a "pending improvements" endorsement which, similar to a "pending disbursements" endorsement issued in connection with a construction loan policy, automatically increases the amount of coverage under the policy in incremental amounts on a periodic basis as improve-ments are completed. The insured would be well advised to consult with the title insurer, at the time of ordering the title commitment for a lease-hold estate, regarding the amount of coverage and the anticipated items of damage in the event of a loss, as the new leasehold endorsements do not provide a specific method for valuing leasehold improvements.

With respect to Tenant Leasehold Improvements that are not com-pleted at the time of the loss, the 2001 Leasehold Endorsements will pay the actual costs incurred for such improvements by the insured up to that date (less the salvage value). This coverage, which is provided under Section 4.g. of the 2001 Leasehold Owner's Endorsement (Section 3.g. in the 2001 Leasehold Loan Endorsement), includes both "hard" and "soft" costs such as "costs incurred to obtain land use, zoning, building and occu-pancy permits, architectural and engineering fees, construction manage-ment fees, costs of environmental testing and reviews, landscaping costs and fees, costs and interest on loans for the acquisition and construction." This is another significant expansion of coverage for insured leasehold owners and lenders.

The 2001 Leasehold Endorsements have added, as Section 1.a., a provision that specifically defines the terms "Evicted" and "Eviction." These terms are defined to mean "the lawful deprivation" of the tenant's right of possession contrary to the terms of the lease, or the lawful prevention of the tenant's use of the land or Tenant Leasehold Improvements for the purposes set forth in the Lease. Thus, if the insured has specified the use of the leased premises and this use, however broad (or narrow), is specified in the lease, the title insurer will be obligated (subject to other terms and conditions of the policy) to insure the tenant against any deprivation of this use. This is yet another important benefit to the insured provided by the 2001 Leasehold Endorsements.

The additional items of damages covered by the 1975 Leasehold Policies, as described earlier in this paper (*i.e.*, removing and relocating Personal Property, damage to such property, and transportation expenses; damages payable to a party having paramount title to that of the lessor under the lease; the amount of rent the insured tenant remains obligated to pay to the landlord after eviction from the Leasehold Estate; and damages incurred by the insured in connection with any sublease) remain basically the same, except that the coverage for transportation of the insured's Personal Property incurred in connection with relocation has been extended from 25 miles to 100 miles. However, Section 4.f. of the 2001 Leasehold Owner's Endorsement (Section 3.f. of the 2001 Leasehold Loan Endorsement) adds an important new item of recoverable loss: "Reasonable costs incurred by the insured to secure a replacement leasehold equivalent to the Leasehold Estate." This further affirms that the "fair market value versus stated lease rental" determination of loss under the 1975 Leasehold Policies is no longer applicable, and constitutes another expansion of coverage.

As mentioned above, a party insured under the 2001 Leasehold Endorsements is entitled to recover (under Section 4.b. of the Leasehold Owner's Endorsement and Section 3.b. of the Leasehold Loan Endorsement) the amount of rent or damages that the tenant is obligated to pay, before eviction, to any person having "paramount title to that of the lessor under the lease." A claim could occur under this provision if, for example, the title policy showed an incorrect party as the landlord and the tenant had been making rent payments to that party instead of the actual owner of the property. Another area in which such a claim might arise is in connection with synthetic leasing transactions. In the typical synthetic lease, the landlord makes no warranties with respect to the condition of title to the property. Therefore, if another person or entity in fact having paramount title to the property were successful in a legal action brought to evict the tenant and hold it accountable for rent that should have been paid to the true titleholder for the period of the tenant's "wrongful" possession, the tenant would have no cause of action against the landlord but would have a claim against the title company for rental amounts that it would be ordered to pay (as well as for any damages it would have to pay because of the termination of any sublease entered into by the tenant).

Furthermore, under Section 4.c. of the Leasehold Owner's Endorsement and Section 3.c. of the Leasehold Loan Endorsement, the insured party is entitled to compensation for loss for the amount of rent that it remains obligated to pay under the lease for the portion of the premises from which it has been evicted. There are relatively few situations in which such a claim is likely to arise. However, the insured party may be able to establish a claim where, for example, the tenant is unable to use the property because of an alleged zoning violation and the title policy contained a zoning endorsement that covered the tenant's intended use of the property. A claim also may arise in connection with a synthetic lease transaction. Rental payments in a synthetic lease are set at a level to provide an uninterrupted stream of income sufficient to service the loan financing for the transaction and a return on the landlord's equity investment. Therefore, the typical synthetic lease is structured as a "triple-net," "bondable," or "hell or high water" lease, *i.e.*, the stipulated rent must continue to be paid by the tenant under virtually all circumstances. As noted above, the landlord in a synthetic lease customarily makes no representation or warranty with respect to the status of title to the property. If the tenant is subsequently evicted as the result of a defect in the landlord's title to the property, the landlord nonetheless may continue to seek to enforce the tenant's obligation to pay rent in order to service the debt on the property. If the tenant has obtained an owner's title policy containing the new 2001 Leasehold Owner's Endorsement, the loss payable will be the difference in the value of the leasehold estate with the defect and without the defect, plus rental payments that the tenant remains obligated to pay notwithstanding the title defect (up to the stated liability amount of the policy), plus additional coverage for the cost of locating and moving to replacement premises (as well as damages suffered by any subtenant of the tenant).

The 2001 Leasehold Endorsements represent a significant improvement in both the scope and substance of title insurance coverage available to leasehold owners and lenders. ALTA, and the title insurers who comprise this organization, have solicited and listened to the concerns of their customers, and have responded to their valuable input. The result is a new leasehold title insurance product that specifically addresses the issues raised by various customer groups. Title insurers have recognized the perceived shortcomings of the 1975 Leasehold Policies, and the need to update and revise existing coverages to meet the demands of an ever-changing commercial real estate environment. By working together to provide comprehensive and practical leasehold title policy endorsements, all parties have benefited — leasehold owners, leasehold lenders, and title insurers.

EXHIBIT A
ENDORSEMENT
ATTACHED TO POLICY NO.
ISSUED BY
First American Title Insurance Company

1. As used in this endorsement, the following terms shall mean:

    a. "Evicted" or "Eviction": (a) the lawful deprivation, in whole or in part, of the right of possession insured by this policy, contrary to the terms of the Lease or (b) the lawful prevention of the use of the land or the Tenant Leasehold Improvements for the purposes permitted by the Lease, in either case, as a result of a matter covered by this policy.

    b. "Lease": the lease agreement described in Schedule A.

    c. "Leasehold Estate": the right of possession for the Lease Term.

    d. "Lease Term": the duration of the Leasehold Estate, including any renewal or extended term if a valid option to renew or extend is contained in the Lease.

    e. "Personal Property": chattels located on the land and property which, because of their character and manner of affixation to the land, can be severed from the land without causing appreciable damage to themselves or to the land to which they are affixed.

    f. "Remaining Lease Term": the portion of the Lease Term remaining after the insured has been Evicted as a result of a matter covered by this policy.

    g. "Tenant Leasehold Improvements": Those improvements, including landscaping, required or permitted to be built on the land by the Lease that have been built at the insured's expense or in which the insured has an interest greater than the right to possession during the Lease Term.

2. The provisions of subsection (b) of Section 7 of the Conditions and Stipulations shall not apply to any Leasehold Estate covered by this policy.

3. Valuation of Estate or Interest Insured

    If, in computing loss or damage, it becomes necessary to value the estates or interests of the insured as the result of a covered matter that results in an Eviction, then that value shall consist of the value for the Remaining Lease Term of the Leasehold Estate and any Tenant Leasehold Improvements existing on the date of the Eviction. The insured claimant shall have the right to have the Leasehold Estate and the Tenant Leasehold Improvements valued either as a whole or separately. In either event, this determination of value shall take into account rent no longer required to be paid for the Remaining Lease Term.

4. Additional Items of Loss Covered by this Endorsement

    If the insured is Evicted, the following items of loss, if applicable, shall be included in computing loss or damage incurred by the insured, but not to the extent that the same are included in the valuation of the estates or interests insured by this policy.

    a. The reasonable cost of removing and relocating any Personal Property that the insured has the right to remove and relocate, situated on the land at the time of Eviction, the cost of transportation of that Personal Property for the initial one hundred miles incurred in connection with the relocation, and the reasonable cost of repairing the Personal Property damaged by reason of the removal and relocation.

    b. Rent or damages for use and occupancy of the land prior to the Eviction which the insured as owner of the Leasehold Estate is obligated to pay to any person having paramount title to that of the lessor in the Lease.

    c. The amount of rent that, by the terms of the Lease, the insured must continue to pay to the lessor after Eviction with respect to the portion of the Leasehold Estate and Tenant Leasehold Improvements from which the insured has been Evicted.

    d. The fair market value, at the time of the Eviction, of the estate or interest of the insured in any lease or sublease made by the insured as lessor of all or part of the Leasehold Estate or the Tenant Leasehold Improvements.

    e. Damages that the insured is obligated to pay to lessees or sublessees on account of the breach of any lease or sublease made by the insured as lessor of all or part of the Leasehold Estate or the Tenant Leasehold Improvements caused by the Eviction.

    f. Reasonable costs incurred by the insured to secure a replacement leasehold equivalent to the Leasehold Estate.

    g. If Tenant Leasehold Improvements are not substantially completed at the time of Eviction, the actual cost incurred by the insured, less the salvage value, for the Tenant Leasehold Improvements up to the time of Eviction. Those costs include costs incurred to obtain land use, zoning, building and occupancy permits, architectural and engineering fees, construction management fees, costs of environmental testing and reviews, landscaping costs and fees, costs and interest on loans for the acquisition and construction.

This endorsement is made a part of the policy and is subject to all of the terms and provisions thereof and of any prior endorsements thereto. Except to the extent expressly stated, it neither modifies any of the terms and provisions of the policy and any prior endorsements, nor does it extend the effective date of the policy and any prior endorsements, nor does it increase the face amount thereof.

First American Title Insurance Company

BY: _____
AUTHORIZED SIGNATORY

ALTA Form 13 (Leasehold — Owner's) — (10-13-01)

ALTA Owner's Policy

EXHIBIT B
ENDORSEMENT
ATTACHED TO POLICY NO.
ISSUED BY
First American Title Insurance Company

1. As used in this endorsement, the following terms shall mean:

    a. "Evicted" or "Eviction": (a) the lawful deprivation, in whole or in part, of the right of possession insured by this policy, contrary to the terms of the Lease or (b) the lawful prevention of the use of the land or the Tenant Leasehold Improvements for the purposes permitted by the Lease, in either case, as a result of a matter covered by this policy.

    b. "Lease": the lease agreement described in Schedule A.

    c. "Leasehold Estate": the right of possession for the Lease Term.

    d. "Lease Term": the duration of the Leasehold Estate, including any renewal or extended term if a valid option to renew or extend is contained in the Lease.

    e. "Personal Property": chattels located on the land and property which, because of their character and manner of affixation to the land, can be severed from the land without causing appreciable damage to themselves or to the land to which they are affixed.

    f. "Remaining Lease Term": the portion of the Lease Term remaining after the insured has been Evicted as a result of a matter covered by this policy.

    g. "Tenant": the tenant under the Lease and, after acquisition of all or any part of the estate or interest in the land described in Schedule A in accordance with the provisions of Section 2(a) of the Conditions and Stipulations of this policy, the insured claimant.

    h. "Tenant Leasehold Improvements": those improvements, including landscaping, required or permitted to be built on the land by the Lease that have been built at the insured's expense or in which the insured has an interest greater than the right to possession during the Lease Term.

2. Valuation of Estate or Interest Insured

    If, in computing loss or damage, it becomes necessary to value the estates or interests insured by this policy as the result of a covered matter that results in an Eviction of the Tenant, then that value shall consist of the value for the Remaining Lease Term of the Leasehold Estate and any Tenant Leasehold Improvements existing on the date of the Eviction. The insured claimant shall have the right to have the Leasehold Estate and the Tenant Leasehold Improvements valued either as a whole or separately. In either event, this determination of value shall take into account rent no longer required to be paid for the Remaining Lease Term.

3. Additional items of loss covered by this endorsement:

    If the insured acquires all or any part of the estate or interest in the land described in Schedule A in accordance with the provisions of Section 2(a) of the Conditions and Stipulations of this policy and thereafter is Evicted, the following items of loss, if applicable, shall be included in computing loss or damage incurred by the insured, but not to the extent that the same are included in the valuation of the estates or interests insured by this policy.

    a. The reasonable cost of removing and relocating any Personal Property that the insured has the right to remove and relocate, situated on the land at the time of Eviction, the cost of transportation of that Personal Property for the initial one hundred miles incurred in connection with the relocation, and the reasonable cost of repairing the Personal Property damaged by reason of the removal and relocation.

    b. Rent or damages for use and occupancy of the land prior to the Eviction which the insured as owner of the Leasehold Estate may be obligated to pay to any person having paramount title to that of the lessor in the Lease.

    c. The amount of rent that, by the terms of the Lease, the insured must continue to pay to the lessor after Eviction with respect to the portion of the Leasehold Estate and Tenant Leasehold Improvements from which the insured has been Evicted.

    d. The fair market value, at the time of the Eviction, of the estate or interest of the insured in any lease or sublease made by Tenant as lessor of all or part of the Leasehold Estate or the Tenant Leasehold Improvements.

    e. Damages that the insured is obligated to pay to lessees or sublessees on account of the breach of any lease or sublease made by the Tenant as lessor of all or part of the Leasehold Estate or the Tenant Leasehold Improvements caused by the Eviction.

    f. Reasonable costs incurred by the insured to secure a replacement leasehold equivalent to the Leasehold Estate.

g. If Tenant Leasehold Improvements are not substantially completed at the time of Eviction, the actual cost incurred by the insured, less the salvage value, for the Tenant Leasehold Improvements up to the time of Eviction. Those costs include costs incurred to obtain land use, zoning, building and occupancy permits, architectural and engineering fees, construction management fees, costs of environmental testing and reviews, and landscaping costs.

This endorsement is made a part of said policy and is subject to all of the terms and provisions thereof and of any prior endorsements thereto. Except to the extent expressly stated, it neither modifies any of the terms and provisions of the policy and any prior endorsements, nor does it extend the effective date of the policy and any prior endorsements, nor does it increase the face amount thereof.

First American Title Insurance Company

BY: _____
AUTHORIZED SIGNATORY

ALTA Form 13.1 (Leasehold — Loan) — (10-13-01)

ALTA Loan Policy

CHAPTER 8
NEGOTIATING LOAN TRANSACTIONS

Robert A. Thompson
Brian D. Smith

---

§ 8.02   LOAN APPLICATION AND COMMITMENTS

[B]   Refundability of Fees

[1]   Application Fees

Page 479, add at end of carryover paragraph:

Increasingly, loan applications include a combination of deposits to be applied to engineering, environmental, legal, accounting/audit, and other due diligence investigation costs and a "Lender Fee" or "Application Fee," which is deemed fully earned upon acceptance of the application.

[C]   Limiting Conditions to Lender's Obligations

[3]   Qualifications of Lender's Right of Approval

Page 484, add to note 4:

The doctrine of good faith and fair dealing has been acknowledged in numerous cases involving "failure to cooperate in the other party's performance" (Restatement of Contracts (Second) § 205, cmt. (d)) and "abuse of a power to determine compliance or to terminate the contract" (Restatement of Contracts (Second) § 205, cmt. (e)).

§ 8.03   LOAN DOCUMENTS

[B]   Promissory Note

[2]   Nonrecourse and Limited Recourse Provisions

[b]   Applicable State Law

Page 504, add to note 12:

See discussion in Restatement of Property (Mortgages) § 4.6, cmt. (i).

[3]   Choice of Law and Forum

Page 505, add to note 13:

For a recent analysis of the enforceability of choice of law provisions in loan documents, *see, e.g.*, Preble, "Choice of Law Opinions: Making the Right Choice," Prob. & Prop. (July/Aug. 1997), at 13.

Page 505, add after subsection [3]:

[4]   "Lock In" and Prepayment Penalty Clauses

Other than being adequately secured and having effective remedies upon loan default, few issues are of greater importance to a permanent lender than maintenance of its anticipated return on its funds. As opposed to construction and land development loans, where the risk to the lender dictates encouragement of the earliest possible repayment and loan fees and other payments, rather than interest, are the primary remuneration, long-term lenders consider a reliable annual yield on investment to be crucial. The primary mechanisms for assuring this objective are "lock-in" clauses and prepayment penalties. The former is nothing more than a prohibition of prepayment for the term of the loan or some shorter specified period; the latter is a provision specifying an amount to be paid to the lender as a condition of full or partial prepayment of the loan.

Lock-in provisions are common in participating loans, where the lender's ability to convert its lien into an ownership interest, and conduit loans, where long-term investment is the premise, rather than simply a benefit, of the transaction. Such provisions appear to be generally enforceable and are, in any event, rarely negotiable. *See* discussion in § **8.06[D]**, this supplement.

Prepayment penalties are often justified as compensation to the lender for costs incurred as a result of loss of a long-term investment opportunity; however, enforceability of such provisions does not appear to depend on that rationale. Requirement for payment of a liquidated sum that bears no relationship to anticipated yield or for prepayment in an interest rate market more favorable to the lender than the stated interest under the existing loan does not appear to affect judicial enforceability. *See* Whitman, "Mortgage Prepayment: A Legal and Economic Analysis," 40 UCLA L. Rev. 851 (1993); Alexander, "Mortgage Prepayment: The Trial of Common Sense," 72 Cornell L. Rev. 288 (1987). Nonetheless, by far the more typical provision in recent loan transactions is a "yield maintenance" provision, which is intended, through a sometimes complex formula, to relate the required payment to the discounted value of the return the lender would have earned over the remaining term of the loan.

Given the importance of the issue to a long-term lender and the general fairness of this approach, such provisions will rarely be negotiable. What is more likely to trigger debate is whether a prepayment penalty should be collectible when repayment is not "voluntary," such as in cases of acceleration upon default, including violation of a due on sale provision, or as a result of casualty loss or condemnation of the real estate collateral.

Negotiation of exemption from a prepayment penalty in the event of loan acceleration upon a default is normally difficult, and arguably of little importance to the borrower. For loans that are (by contract or as a result of state anti-deficiency legislation) non-recourse, prepayment penalties are simply one more obligation of the borrower that cannot be collected. For recourse loans, the issue may be almost as academic.

Some courts have invalidated prepayment fees in the context of acceleration for violation of "due on sale" provisions, on the grounds that such prepayment is "involuntary." *See Tam v. California Fed. Sav. & Loan Ass'n*, 140 Cal. App. 3d 800, 189 Cal. Rptr. 775 (1983); *Slevin Container Corp. v. Provident Fed. Sav. & Loan Ass'n*, 98 Ill. App. 3d 646, 424 N.E.2d 939 (1981); Restatement of Property (Mortgages) § 6.3, Reporters' Note. Most lenders would disagree that transfer to a third party or to the lender by foreclosure is not within the control of the borrower, and again consider the issue to be non-negotiable.

It is with respect to acceleration or partial prepayment of the loan upon casualty loss or condemnation that the borrower's counsel is on strongest ground. If the loan documents are silent on the issue, common law generally nullifies application of prepayment fees in such circumstances. Assuming that the lender is not obligated by local law or provisions in the loan documents to apply insurance or condemnation proceeds to restoration of the real estate collateral (*see* **§ 8.03[C][7]**, *infra*, this supplement), courts have barred the imposition of prepayment fees on such amounts as are used to reduce or retire the debt. Restatement of Property (Mortgages) § 6.3. The reasoning of those decisions supports an argument by the borrower's attorney that, in the event that insurance or condemnation proceeds are insufficient to restore the premises, a prepayment penalty on down payment of the loan is not only truly involuntary, but also inequitable.

[C]   Mortgage or Deed of Trust and Loan Agreement

[2]   Dragnet and Spreader Clauses

Page 508, add new note 13.1 at end of second full paragraph:

[13.1] In most jurisdictions, dragnet clauses are enforceable and afford priority over subsequent lien holders only to the extent that future advances are either specifically described or, if generally referred to, are "similar in character" to the initial loan. *See* Restatement of Property (Mortgages) § 2.4, and articles and cases cited therein.

Page 509, add to note 14:

The law of fixtures or the "doctrine of accession" generally operates to include after-acquired improvements and fixtures as part of the original real estate collateral in a secured loan, even if the loan documents are silent on the issue. *See, e.g.,* 1 G. Nelson & D. Whitman, Real Estate Finance Law § 9.3 (3d ed. 1993). Accordingly, any intent to segregate such interests for separate financing or other purposes must be expressly stated in the loan documents.

[6]   Extraordinary Risks

Page 527, add note 38.1 at end of carryover paragraph:

Industry reactions to the events of September 11, 2001, well illustrate both how quickly postures can change in the realm of extraordinary risks and how high are the stakes of the negotiations. At this writing, insurance against the consequences of acts of terrorism is either unavailable or economically utterly infeasible. Yet, a number of lenders have issued demands for the immediate addition of terrorism insurance, without reference to the market reality and under the auspices of their contract entitlement to dictate insurance requirements. Absent the kinds of constraints to customary provisions or commercial reasonableness discussed above (or some legislative intervention—through a combination of governmental coverage, requirements for private coverage or the denial of lender's rights to insist on such coverage), the posture of a borrower faced with such lender demands, however impractical, is, at best, uncertain.

[7]   Insurance Proceeds and Condemnation Awards

Page 528, add to note 39:

In most jurisdictions, express provisions in loan documents providing for payment of insurance and condemnation proceeds to the lender are enforceable. *See* Restatement of Property (Mortgages) § 4.7. The Restatement, however, notes the "harshness" of such provisions, and suggests that, unless specifically provided to the contrary, such proceeds should be made available for restoration of the real estate collateral, subject to reasonable conditions protective of the lender's interest. Such an approach is typically negotiated and expressly provided in loan documents, as described below in this section. The Restatement also notes, in § 4.7, cmt. (e), that a mortgagor's waiver of the right to use funds for restoration may be unenforceable if the facts and circumstances indicate a violation of the mortgagee's duty of good faith and fair dealing. *See* § **8.02[C][3]**, *supra*, this supplement.

[15]   Subordination Provisions

Page 549, add to note 47:

The Restatement of Property (Mortgages) § 7.7, summarizes the state of the law in most jurisdictions, noting generally that to be enforceable against an existing lender a subordination covenant must describe the subordinating loan with "reasonable specificity." Comment (b) to § 7.7 provides illustrations of the principle.

[D] Assignment of Leases

[2] Assignment Language

Page 553, add to note 49:

There has been considerable scholarly commentary on the alternative legal characterizations of an assignment of rents, the effect of specific language in loan documents, the point in time when a lender can effect a remedy and the nature of that remedy, and analysis of cases that are frequently adjudicated by federal Bankruptcy Courts interpreting state law. *See* Restatement of Property (Mortgages) § 4.2. In most jurisdictions, whatever the technical analysis, an assignment of rents is collectable only upon default by the mortgagor under the loan documents, and judicially enforceable only by application for appointment of a receiver for the real property collateral.

§ 8.06   PARTICIPATION LOANS

[D]   Relationship to Prepayment Rights

Page 591, add new note 57.1 at end of second to last sentence of first full paragraph:

[57.1] Prepayment penalties are generally enforceable in most jurisdictions. *See* discussion in **§ 8.03[B][4]**, this supplement. In comment (c) to the Restatement of Property (Mortgages) § 6.2, it is argued that, in view of the enforceability of "lock in" provisions and the ability of the mortgagor to avoid the sanction, the size of the prepayment penalty should be irrelevant. The same comment acknowledges that in certain circumstances (presumably only in the case of "involuntary" default) enforcement of such a penalty might violate principles of unconscionability or the duty of good faith and fair dealing.

§ 8.07   SECURITIZED LOANS

[D]   Release/Defeasance

Page 595, add new note 59.1 at end of second sentence of the second full paragraph:

[59.1] The recent phenomenon of defeasance provisions in conduit loan transactional documents is reciprocal to a much more venerable, but little acknowledged, principle of common law that allows the mortgagee, as a matter of right, to substitute collateral, equal in value to the debt (and other loan fees and costs), that is the substantial equivalent to cash. *See* discussion, articles, and cases cited in Restatement of Property (Mortgages) § 6.2, cmt. (e). Express defeasance provisions, of course, spell out the lender's right to require replacement collateral and additional protections; it is unclear whether the borrower's common law right to release the lien on its property and substitute collateral (which need not be stated in the documents) would provide a more generous right to the mortgagee or whether a court would enforce this common law right in a commercial context, in which the loan documents express, in quite numbing detail, the parties' intent as to their respective rights and obligations. In any event, such a right need not be stated in the loan documents and would likely be resisted by the lender if it were suggested by the borrower.

CHAPTER 9
OPINION LETTERS IN REAL ESTATE LOAN TRANSACTIONS

Joel J. Goldberg
Robert T. Flick

§ 9.02 OPINION LETTER REFERENCE MATERIALS — BAR COMMITTEE REPORTS

Page 605, add at end of section:

Bar associations have continued to publish updates to their reports, which have continued to increase the body of knowledge of opinion letter content but have not served to increase the use of standardized opinion formats. *See* **§ 9.15**, this supplement.

§ 9.11 QUALIFICATIONS

[C] Practical Realization Approach

Page 626, replace note 32 with:

[32] Lawrence G. Preble, "The Remedies Opinion Revisited: A Primer for Real Estate Lawyers" 33 Real Prop., Prob. & Tr. J. 63, 80 (Spring 1998) (hereinafter Preble).

§ 9.15 OPINION PRACTICE/CONDUCT

Page 641, add at end of section:

The impact of model opinions and bar committee opinion reports on opinion practice has been significant and beneficial. Through such widely promulgated opinions and reports, opinion givers and recipients (and their clients) have gained a better appreciation of the purpose of opinions, the meaning of important words commonly found in opinions, and highlighted the pros and cons of using a laundry list or generic qualification approach to identify qualifications to and limitations of the enforceability opinion.

The impact of such opinions and reports on opinion content, however, has been less significant. Contrary to the intent of the model opinion report authors, opinion givers still do not customarily deliver, nor do opinion recipients or their counsel customarily require, an opinion on all or substantially all the terms of a model opinion promulgated by a bar association or similar group. In fact, for many opinion givers, model opinions merely have been a source for more qualifications, exceptions, and other limitations to be incorporated in long-used personal opinion forms. As one commentator has noted: "Is the laundry list dead? Not yet — and it is probably not even endangered. To many lawyers, an extensive laundry list is evidence of their experience and sophistication and the temptation to add one more exception is irresistible." Preble at 87.

Although model opinions and opinion reports have had some effect on the content of opinions, perhaps the greatest impact of the promulgation of model opinions and opinion committee reports, the increase in articles and seminars concerning opinion practice and increased discussion of legal opinions has been the welcome and noticeable increase in the professionalism of opinion practice. With respect to general real estate practice, one commentator has noted that a real estate practitioner must be a "successful facilitator" to make a transaction possible and close a deal. Peter W. Salsich, Jr., "Professionalism for the Real Estate Law Practitioner," 36 Real Prop., Prob. & Tr. J. 593, 597 (Fall 2001). In addition to the increased civility of opinion practice, benefits of such increased professionalism include opinions produced promptly and at lower cost, due to the more appropriate expectations and stated needs of the opinion recipient, an increased understanding by the opinion giver of the real needs of the opinion recipient, and the resulting shorter time required for the opinion giver and recipient to reach agreement on the terms of the opinion.

Identification of opinion principles and guidelines has not been a recent development, but more recently opinion givers and recipients have realized that adherence to such matters is more likely to lead to prompt, civil, and reasonable opinions and opinion negotiations than is focusing on particular opinion forms. The New York Report, for example, identifies and emphasizes the following principles:

1. The purpose, scope and text of an opinion should be addressed as early as possible.

2. The focus of the opinion should be primarily on matters outside the knowledge of the lender's counsel (such as opinions with respect to the borrower's status and authority and compliance with law and other agreements) and on the remedies opinion.

3. Lender's counsel should not ask for an opinion such counsel would not be willing to give in similar circumstances.

4. The burden on the borrower's counsel of doing due diligence should not be disproportionate to the benefit to the lender.

5. It is not appropriate to ask for an unqualified opinion on an uncertain legal principle.

6. Counsel for both parties should assume that their clients desire to enter into an enforceable agreement. If an important legal issue is encountered, the transaction should be restructured, if possible, to remove any legal uncertainty. Important issues should not be ignored or concealed by broadly stated exceptions and qualification to an opinion.

New York Report at 123–24.

Although stated in 1998 in the New York Report, the principles appeared with less detail in the 1989 Mortgage Loan Opinion Report prepared by the Committee on Real Property Law of the Association of the Bar of the City of New York and the Real Property Law Section of the New York State Bar Association.

Many others have also advocated adherence to principles and guidelines regarding opinion practice. For example, in 2002 the Committee on Legal Opinions of the Section on Business Law of the American Bar Association promulgated the *Guidelines for Preparation of Closing Opinions*. 57 Bus. Law. 875 (2002). Although the Guidelines, like the Accord, did not address all areas of concern and importance to opinion givers and opinion recipients in a real estate secured loan transaction, they are valuable for their overall perspective and promulgation of generally applicable opinion letter principles. More recently, The American College of Real Estate Lawyers (ACREL) and the Real Property, Probate and Trust Law Section of the American Bar Association adopted the *Real Estate*

Opinion Letter Guidelines. 38 Real Prop., Prob. & Tr. J. 241 (Summer 2003) (the Guidelines). The ACREL guidelines provide technical guidance as to the content of opinions, such as the implications of the use of the phrase "to our knowledge," and also contain general benchmarks for the opinion process and the conduct of counsel, such as the following:

1. The benefit of an opinion to the recipient should warrant the time and expense to prepare it. Guidelines at 244.

2. Opinion requests should be limited to matters that are reasonably related to the transaction. *Id.* at 245.

3. Early in the negotiation of the transaction documents, counsel for the opinion recipient should specify the opinions the opinion recipient wishes to receive. *Id.* at 247.

4. An opinion giver should not be asked to render an opinion that counsel for the opinion recipient would not render if it were the opinion giver and possessed the requisite expertise. Similarly, an opinion giver should not refuse to render an opinion that lawyers experienced in the matters under consideration would commonly render in comparable situations. *Id.* at 248.

A sample legal opinion is included in this supplement as **Appendix 9C**. The sample opinion is neither a lender's form opinion nor a borrower's counsel's form opinion, but an example of a negotiated legal opinion that was delivered and accepted in an actual transaction. Consistent with the provisions of **§ 9.06** in the main volume, the opining law firm had lawyers admitted to practice in each of the jurisdictions whose law was expressly addressed in the opinion, and such lawyers participated in the negotiation and approval of the opinion.

This sample opinion, which addresses some topics not considered in the preceding provisions of this chapter (e.g., the perfection of security interests and guaranty and suretyship issues), is included merely as an example of a legal opinion and is not intended to serve as an "illustrative," "standard," "form," or "model" opinion. Further, although the sample opinion contains some opinion items, qualifications, and assumptions common to many opinions, it may not be appropriate in other transactions or typical of opinions delivered in all jurisdictions. The sample opinion, together with the balance of this chapter, should provide some guidance in negotiating legal opinions.

Page 641, add new section after § 9.15:

§ 9.16   STANDARDIZATION VERSUS CUSTOMARY PRACTICE

Over recent decades, the Accord and other attempts to standardize opinion letters have not gained the acceptance envisioned when such reports and opinions were first promulgated. In place of a desire to simplify opinion practice by adopting uniform opinions there is a recognition that opinion practice is often a creature of "customary practice" and that customary opinion practice may vary over time, and by region. Guidelines, as discussed in § **9.15**, this supplement, are an important and major component of "customary practice." As stated in the Legal Opinion Principles promulgated by the ABA Committee on Legal Opinions, "guidelines are frequently looked to for guidance regarding customary legal opinion practice." "Legal Opinion Principles," 53 Bus. Law. 831, 831 (1998).

"Customary practice" and similar terms are not "precise." In defining "customary practice," the TriBar Committee states that a consensus has developed regarding the meaning of language used in opinion letters, as well as the nature and scope of factual and legal investigation required to support particular opinions. "Third Party Closing Opinions: A Report of the TriBar Committee," 53 Bus. Law. 591, 595 (1998). For the TriBar Committee, customary practice is a starting point, allowing for communication without lengthy descriptions of the diligence process, detailed descriptions of terms, and laborious recitals of assumptions and exceptions. *Id.* at 600. As stated in the *Restatement (Third) of the Law Governing Lawyers*, custom and practice enable opinion givers to give abbreviated opinions that facilitate closings as certain assumptions, limitations, and standards of diligence are understood between counsel and not included in the opinion. *Restatement (Third) of the Law: The Law Governing Lawyers* § 95, Reporter's Note, cmt. c (2000). Custom and practice may be determined by considering such things as local practice, bar association reports, and articles.

The principles at the core of customary practice do not provide a form of opinion; but, rather, provide a general format, means, and approach to guide the opinion delivery process. It is likely that opinion givers and counsel to opinion recipients will continue to follow and enhance general behavioral guidelines concerning the opinion process. It remains to be seen, however, whether opinion givers will use customary practice simply to modify or perhaps embellish opinions stated in opinions, or ultimately will give opinions based on customary terms and expectations not expressly stated in the opinion.

APPENDIX 9A
RELEVANT REPORTS

Page 644, add before "Pennsylvania":

North Carolina

Report of the Opinion Letter Subcommittee of the Commercial Law Committee of the Real Property Section of the North Carolina Bar Association (May 1993).

Report of the Legal Opinion Committee of the Business Law Section of the North Carolina Bar Association, "Third Party Legal Opinions in Business Transactions" (January 1, 1999).

Page 645, add at end of appendix:

Washington

Report on Third Party Legal Opinion Practice in the State of Washington by the Ad Hoc Committee on Third-Party Legal Opinions of the Business Law Section of the Washington State Bar Association (Fall 1998).

Page 647, add new appendix:

APPENDIX 9C
SAMPLE LEGAL OPINION

[LAW FIRM LETTERHEAD]

[DATE]

_____

_____

_____

Re: $_____ Loan from _____ ("Lender") to _____ ("Borrower") concerning _____ (the "Project")

Ladies and Gentlemen:

A. **Introduction.**

We have acted as special counsel to Borrower, _____, a _____ ("Recourse Guarantor"), _____, a _____ ("General Partner"), _____, a _____ ("Managing Member"), and _____, a _____ ("Property Manager"), in connection with the $_____loan ("Loan") to be made by Lender to Borrower pursuant to the terms and conditions of the Loan Documents (as defined below). This opinion is furnished to you pursuant to the request of Borrower. Capitalized terms which are used herein and are not otherwise defined herein shall have the meanings set forth in the Loan Documents.

B. **Documents and Items Reviewed.**

For purposes of rendering our opinions set forth herein, we have reviewed originals or copies of the following documents, each dated as of _____ _____, 200__:

1. Promissory Note (the "Note") made payable by the Borrower to the order of _____ (the "Lender") in the principal amount of $_____;

2. Deed of Trust, Security Agreement, Financing Statement, Fixture Filing, and Assignment of Leases, Rents, and Security Deposits made by Borrower to a trustee for the benefit of Lender (the "Deed of Trust");

3. Assignment of Leases, Rents, and Security Deposits from the Borrower to Lender (the "Assignment of Leases and Rents");

4. Account Security, Pledge, Assignment, and Control Agreement made by and among Borrower, Lender, and Property Manager (the "Account Agreement");

5. Lockbox Account Control Acknowledgment Agreement made by and between Borrower and _____ Bank, N.A. (the "Lockbox Agreement");

6. Manager's Consent and Subordination of Management Agreement made by Borrower and Property Manager to Lender (the "Manager's Subordination Agreement");

7. Environment Indemnity made by Recourse Guarantor to Lender (the "Environmental Indemnity");

8. Guaranty of Recourse Obligations made by Recourse Guarantor to Lender (the "Recourse Guaranty");

9. Uniform Commercial Code Financing Statements from the Borrower, as debtor, to Lender, as secured party (the "Financing Statements");

10. Rate Cap Pledge and Security Agreement from the Borrower to Lender ("RC Pledge Agreement"); and

11. Rate Cap Uniform Commercial Code Financing Statements from the Borrower, as debtor, to Lender, as secured party (the "RC Financing Statements").

The Deed of Trust, the Assignment of Leases and Rents, the Manager's Subordination Agreement, the Account Agreement, the Lockbox Agreement, the RC Pledge Agreement, the RC Financing Statements, and the Financing Statements are hereinafter collectively referred to as the "Security Documents." The Security Documents, together with the Note, the Environmental Indemnity, and the Recourse Guaranty, are hereinafter collectively referred to as the "Loan Documents."

In rendering our opinion we have also examined such certificates of public officials as we have deemed necessary for the purpose of our opinions herein expressed in Section D.1 below. With respect to our opinions set forth in Sections D.6(c) and (d) and D.14 below, we have relied solely upon, with your permission, our knowledge and that certain Borrower's Certificate attached hereto as Exhibit A and incorporated herein by reference ("Borrower's Certificate").

When we render a statement or opinion "to our knowledge" or concerning an item "known to us," or use words of similar import, such statement or opinion is based solely upon (a) the current, actual knowledge, without duty to investigate, of the attorneys within this firm who have given substantive legal attention to the representation of Borrower in connection with the Loan; (b) the contents of the Borrower's Certificate; and (c) such other investigation, if any, as may be specifically identified in this opinion letter.

C. **Assumptions.**

In rendering the opinions contained in this opinion letter, we have assumed, with your permission and without independent investigation or verification, that:

1. All natural persons involved in the Loan have sufficient legal capacity to enter into and perform their respective obligations under the Loan Documents or to carry out their roles with respect to the Loan.

2. Each party to the Loan other than Borrower, Property Manager, and Recourse Guarantor has satisfied all legal requirements that are applicable to it to the extent necessary to make the Loan Documents enforceable against it.

3. Each of the parties to the Loan other than Borrower, Property Manager, and Recourse Guarantor has complied with all legal requirements pertaining to its status as such status relates to its rights to enforce the Loan Documents.

4. Borrower holds the requisite title and rights to any property involved in the Loan that is designated as belonging to Borrower, including, without limitation, any property that is designated as collateral or security for the performance of the obligations of Borrower under the Loan Documents.

5. The conduct of each of the parties to the Loan complies with any and all applicable requirements of good faith, fair dealing, and conscionability.

6. There has not been any mutual mistake of fact, fraud, duress, or undue influence.

7. All statutes, judicial and administrative decisions, and rules and regulations of governmental agencies, applicable to this opinion, are generally available to lawyers practicing in the States of California and New York and are in a format that makes legal research reasonably feasible.

8. Each party to the Loan Documents other than Borrower, Recourse Guarantor, and Property Manager has full power and authority to execute, deliver, and perform such Loan Documents, and each party to the Loan Documents other than Borrower, Recourse Guarantor, and Property Manager has duly authorized the execution, delivery, and performance of such Loan Documents by all necessary action.

9. All documents submitted to us as originals are authentic, and all documents submitted to us as certified, conformed, or photostatic copies conform to authentic original documents.

10. The descriptions of the real property and the personal property contained in the Loan Documents are legally sufficient and adequate under applicable law (including, without limitation, the Uniform Commercial Code, as presently in effect in the State of California or the State of New York ("UCC")) to enable a subsequent purchaser or mortgagee to identify such property.

11. The terms and conditions of the Loan as reflected in the Loan Documents have not been amended, modified, or supplemented by any other written agreement or written understanding of the parties or written waiver of any of the material provisions of the Loan Documents. To our knowledge, without independent investigation, nothing has come to our attention that leads us to believe that we are not justified in making the foregoing assumption.

12. Except for such consents, approvals, authorizations, registrations, declarations, and filings as have heretofore been obtained or made, no consents or approvals of, authorizations by, or registrations, declarations, or filings with any governmental authority are required for any party, other than Borrower, Recourse Guarantor, or Property Manager, to execute, deliver, or perform its obligations under the Loan Documents to which it is a party.

13. The Deed of Trust and the Financing Statements will be recorded and filed, as applicable, with the County Recorder of the county in which the Property is located and with the California Secretary of State, and all recordation or filing charges specified herein will be paid thereon.

14. Lender has given "value" (as defined in the California Commercial Code ("CCC") and in the New York Commercial Code) to the Borrower for the Note and for the security interests granted under the Loan Documents.

15. All tangible personal property of Borrower in which a security interest is granted under the Loan Documents (other than accounts or goods of a type normally used in more than one jurisdiction) is located at the Property.

D. **Opinions.**

Based on the foregoing and upon such investigation as we have deemed necessary, and subject to the qualifications and exceptions herein contained, we are of the opinion that:

1.(a) The Borrower is a limited partnership duly organized, validly existing, and in good standing under the laws of the State of Delaware and is authorized to do business and in good standing in the State of California. Borrower has the requisite power to own its properties and to carry on its business as now being conducted.

(b) Recourse Guarantor is a corporation, duly organized, validly existing, and in good standing under the laws of the State of Maryland and is authorized to do business and in good standing in the State of California.

(c) The Property Manager is a corporation, duly organized, validly existing, and in good standing under the laws of the State of Maryland and is authorized to do business and is in good standing in the State of California.

(d) The General Partner is a limited liability company, duly organized, validly existing, and in good standing under the laws of the State of Delaware and is authorized to do business and is in good standing in the State of California.

(e) The Managing Member is a limited partnership, duly authorized, validly existing, and in good standing under the laws of the State of Delaware.

2. Under the Delaware Revised Uniform Limited Partnership Act, 6 Del. C. Sec. 17-101 *et seq.*, (the "ALP Act") and the limited partnership agreement of Borrower ("Borrower's LP Agreement"), Borrower has all necessary limited partnership power and authority to execute and deliver the Loan Documents to which Borrower is party, and to perform all of Borrower's obligations thereunder. Under the LP Act and the Borrower's LP Agreement, the execution and delivery by Borrower of the Loan Documents to which Borrower is a party, and the performance by Borrower of its obligations thereunder, have been duly authorized by all necessary limited partnership action on the part of Borrower.

3. The transfer of the Project to Borrower by Managing Member has been duly authorized by all necessary limited liability company, partnership, and corporate action, as applicable, and no consent from any of the constituent limited partners of Managing Member is required with respect to the transfer of the Project from Managing Member to Borrower or the execution and delivery of the Loan Documents by Borrower or Recourse Guarantor or the performance by Borrower or Recourse Guarantor of their respective obligations under the Loan Documents.

4. The execution and delivery of the Environmental Indemnity and the Recourse Guaranty by the Recourse Guarantor have been duly authorized by all necessary limited liability company, partnership, and corporate action, as applicable.

5. The execution and delivery of the Manager's Subordination Agreement by Property Manager have been duly authorized by all necessary limited liability company, partnership, and corporate action, as applicable.

6. The execution, delivery, and performance by the Borrower and Recourse Guarantor of the Loan Documents to which it is a party does not (a) conflict with or result in a breach of any of the terms, conditions, or provisions of, or constitute a default under, the partnership agreement, partnership certificate, articles of incorporation, by-laws, trust agreement, or trust certificate, as applicable, of the Borrower or Recourse Guarantor; (b) contravene any law, statute, or regulation of the United States of America or the States of New York or California; (c) violate any order, writ, injunction, or decree of which we have knowledge, issued by any court or governmental authority of the United States of America or the States of New York or California or any agency or political subdivision of any of them to which the Borrower or Recourse Guarantor is subject; or (d) to our knowledge, conflict with or result in any breach of any of the terms or provisions of, or constitute a default under, or result in the creation or imposition of (or the obligation to create or impose) any lien other than the lien of the Deed of Trust and the Assignment of Leases and Rents upon any of the assets or properties of the Borrower or Recourse Guarantor pursuant to the terms of any material indenture, mortgage, deed of trust, agreement, contract, or instrument known to us to which the Borrower or Recourse Guarantor is a party or by which it or any of its assets or properties is bound.

7. The Loan Documents to which Borrower is a party are the valid and binding obligations of Borrower, enforceable against Borrower in accordance with their respective terms.

8. The Environmental Indemnity and the Recourse Guaranty are the legal, valid, and binding obligations of the Recourse Guarantor, enforceable against the Recourse Guarantor in accordance with their terms.

9. The Manager's Subordination Agreement is the legal, valid, and binding obligation of the Property Manager, enforceable against the Property Manager in accordance with its terms.

10. The Deed of Trust is in form sufficient to create a lien on the real property collateral described therein ("Deed of Trust Collateral") in favor of the trustee thereunder for the benefit of the beneficiary thereunder, and the Financing Statements and the RC Financing Statements are in form sufficient to create and perfect a security interest in favor of Lender as secured party, with respect to those items of collateral described in the Financing Statements or the RC Financing Statements in which a security interest may be perfected by filing ("UCC Collateral"), in each case to secure the full amount of the secured obligations described in the Deed of Trust. In order to provide constructive notice of the lien created by the Deed of Trust and in order to perfect the security interest created by the Financing Statements or the RC Financing Statements with respect to the UCC Collateral, it is necessary to record the Deed of Trust in the Official Records of _____ County, State of California, and to file the Financing Statements in the office of the California Secretary of State pursuant to the recording and filing systems established pursuant to applicable California law. Regarding fixtures included in the UCC Collateral, we have assumed that such fixtures are located on the Deed of Trust Collateral and that the Borrower had or will have an interest of record in the Deed of Trust Collateral at the time of filing and recording of such Fixture Filing. Except for the filing of periodic continuation statements as required by the UCC and except for the recording of a Notice of Intent to Preserve Security Interest pursuant to California Civil Code Sections 880.310 880.370, it is not necessary to re-record, re-register, or re-file the Deed of Trust or the Financing Statement or to record, register, or file any other or additional documents, instruments, or statements in order to maintain the priority of the liens and security interests created thereby; provided, however, that additional financing statements and fixture filings may be required to be filed if Borrower changes its name, identity, or corporate structure, or the jurisdiction in which its place of business (or, if it has more than one place of business, its chief executive office) or the UCC Collateral is located. There are no mortgage taxes or filing fees payable upon the recording and filing of such document except: (i) nominal recording and filing fees payable to the County Recorder of _____ County, California, and to the California Secretary of State in connection therewith; (ii) any transfer taxes

assessed in connection with any transfer of the Deed of Trust Collateral or interest therein (other than the transfer that occurs upon the execution and delivery of the Deed of Trust); and (iii) any fee or charge payable to any entity whose services may have been used to assist in such recordation and filing. We express no opinion, however, with respect to any income, franchise, sales, withholding, real or personal property, business license, or other tax that may result from the transactions contemplated by the Loan Documents or the performance of the obligations described therein, including the payment of the indebtedness secured by the Deed of Trust.

11. The Assignment of Leases and Rents is in proper form so as to comply with the recording requirements of the State of California.

12. After the due execution and delivery of the Deed of Trust by Borrower and the unconditional funding of the Loan by Lender, the Deed of Trust will create a lien upon the real property portion of the Deed of Trust Collateral. After the due execution and delivery of the Security Instrument and the Financing Statements, and upon the proper filing of the Financing Statements in the Office of the Secretary of State of the State of California, the security interest created by the Security Instrument and the Financing Statements in the UCC Collateral will be perfected to the extent a security interest in the UCC Collateral can be perfected by the filing of a UCC-1 financing statement in the State of California under the provisions of the UCC.

13. After the due execution and delivery of the RC Pledge and the RC Financing Statements, and upon the proper filing of the RC Financing Statements in the Office of the Secretary of State of the State of New York, the security interest created by the RC Pledge and the RC Financing Statements in the collateral described therein will be perfected to the extent a security interest in such collateral can be perfected by the filing of a UCC-1 financing statement in the State of New York under the provisions of the UCC.

14. The Account Agreement is effective to create in favor of Lender a valid security interest under the Uniform Commercial Code in effect in the State of New York on the date hereof (the "NY UCC") (including the NY UCC as made applicable to any security entitlements with respect to book-entry securities (as such term is defined in 31 CFR § 357.2) pursuant to 31 CFR § 357.11) in all of Borrower's right, title, and interest in the security entitlements in the accounts listed on <u>Exhibit B</u> attached hereto (the "Security Accounts"). "Security entitlement" has the meaning set forth in § 8-102(a)(17) of the UCC with respect to "financial assets" (as defined in § 8-102(a)(9) of the UCC) and the meaning set forth in 31 CFR § 357.2 with respect to "book-entry securities" (as defined in 31 CFR § 357.2).

15. Based solely upon our review of our firm's internal litigation docket and the Borrower's Certificate, we have no knowledge of any pending or threatened litigation or proceedings against Borrower, Recourse

Guarantor, Property Manager, Managing Member, or General Partner concerning the Project.

16.   The State of California has no law pursuant to which a lien against any assets or properties of Borrower (whether real, personal, mixed, tangible, or intangible) superior to the lien created by the Deed of Trust could arise as a result of a violation of environmental laws or regulations of such State. No environmental law or regulation of the State of California would require any remedial or removal action or certification of nonapplicability as a condition to the granting of the Deed of Trust, the foreclosure or other enforcement of the Security Documents, or the sale of any assets or properties of Borrower (whether real, personal, mixed, tangible, or intangible) located in the State of California; provided, however, that:

   a.   We assume for purposes of the opinion contained in this sentence that the Project is not a "border zone property" or "hazardous waste property" as defined and used in California Health & Safety Code Sections 25220 through 25241 and is not and will not be otherwise subject to classification or restriction under those sections (to our knowledge, based solely upon our review of the Borrower's Certificate, the Project has not previously been designated as a "border zone property" or a "hazardous waste property");

   b.   We note that certain disclosures regarding the presence or release of hazardous substances are required under California law in connection with a proposed conveyance or lease of real property, including, without limitation, under California Health & Safety Code Section 25359.7, and that such disclosures could cause a prospective purchaser or lender, as a practical matter, to condition its purchase of, or loan secured by, the Project upon the prior completion of remediation or removal activities or a certification of nonapplicability with respect to the Project (to our knowledge, based solely upon our review of the Borrower's Certificate, no such disclosure has been given by Borrower to Lender); and

   c.   We note that certain notifications regarding the release of hazardous substances are required under California law, including, without limitation, under the California Environmental Responsibility Act (California Civil Code Section 850 et seq.), and that such notifications could cause a prospective purchaser or lender, as a practical matter, to condition its purchase of, or loan secured by, the Project upon the prior completion of remediation or removal activities or a certification of nonapplicability with respect to the Project (to our knowledge, based solely upon our review of the Borrower's Certificate, no such notification has been given by Borrower to Lender).

17. Except as expressly referenced in this opinion letter, no approval, authorization, or other action by, or filing with, any governmental authority of the United States of America or the States of California or New York is required for the valid execution or delivery by the Borrower of any of the Loan Documents or the performance by Borrower of its payment obligations thereunder.

18. The Loan, as made, will not violate any applicable usury laws of the State of California, assuming for the purposes of this opinion that the internal laws of the State of California were applied.

19. The Loan, as made, will not violate any applicable usury laws of the State of New York, assuming for the purposes of this opinion that the internal laws of the State of New York were applied.

E. **Bankruptcy and Insolvency Exception.**

Our opinions are subject to the effect of bankruptcy, insolvency, reorganization, receivership, moratorium, and other similar laws affecting the rights and remedies of creditors generally. This exception includes, without limitation:

1. The Federal Bankruptcy Code and thus comprehends, among others, matters of turn-over, automatic stay, avoiding powers, fraudulent transfer, preference, discharge, conversion of a non-recourse obligation into a recourse claim, limitations on ipso facto and anti-assignment clauses, and the coverage of pre-petition security agreements applicable to property acquired after a petition is filed;

2. All other Federal and state bankruptcy, insolvency, reorganization, receivership, moratorium, arrangement, and assignment for the benefit of creditors laws that affect the rights and remedies of creditors generally (not just creditors of specific types of debtors);

3. State fraudulent transfer and fraudulent conveyance laws; and

4. Judicially developed doctrines relevant to any of the foregoing laws (but excluding the substantive consolidation of entities, which is covered in a separate opinion).

F. **Equitable Principles Limitation.**

Our opinions are subject to the effect of general principles of equity, whether applied by a court of law or equity. This limitation includes, without limitation, the following principles:

1. Governing the availability of specific performance, injunctive relief, or other equitable remedies, which generally place the award of such remedies, subject to certain guidelines, in the discretion of the court to which application for such relief is made;

2. Affording equitable defenses (e.g., waiver, laches, and estoppel) against a party seeking enforcement;

3. Requiring good faith and fair dealing in the performance and enforcement of a contract by the party seeking its enforcement;

4. Requiring commercial reasonableness in the performance and enforcement of an agreement by the party seeking enforcement of the contract; and

5. Affording defenses based upon the unconscionability of the enforcing party's conduct after the parties have entered into the contract.

G. **Generic Exception and Assurance.**

Certain remedies, waivers, and other provisions of the Loan Documents may not be enforceable; nevertheless, subject to the limitations expressed elsewhere in this opinion, upon a material default by Borrower in the payment of principal or interest thereon as provided in the Note or upon a material default by the Borrower in the performance of any other material covenant of the Loan Documents, such unenforceability will not preclude (1) the acceleration of the obligation of the Borrower to repay such principal and interest, (2) enforcement in accordance with applicable law of the assignment of rents set forth in the Loan Documents, (3) the foreclosure in accordance with applicable law of the security interests in the described collateral created by the Loan Documents, and (4) judicial enforcement in accordance with applicable law of the obligation of Borrower to repay such principal or interest as provided in the Note.

H. **Additional Qualifications.**

To the extent the law of the State of California or the State of New York applies any of the following rules to one or more of the provisions of a Loan Document, our opinion is subject to the effect of generally applicable rules of law that:

1. Limit or affect the enforcement of provisions of a contract that purport to require waiver of the obligations of good faith, fair dealing, and commercial reasonableness;

2. Provide the forum selection clauses in contracts are not necessarily binding on the court(s) in the forum selected;

3. Limit the availability of a remedy under certain circumstances where another remedy has been elected;

4. Limit the right of a creditor to use force or cause a breach of the peace in enforcing rights;

5. Relate to the sale or disposition of collateral or the requirements of a commercially reasonable sale;

6. Limit the enforceability of provisions releasing, exculpating, or exempting a party from, or requiring indemnification of a party for, liability for its own action or inaction, to the extent the action or inaction involves gross negligence, recklessness, willful misconduct, or unlawful conduct;

7. May, where less than all of a contract may be unenforceable, limit the enforceability of the balance of the contract to circumstances in which the unenforceable portion is not an essential part of the agreed exchange;

8. Govern and afford judicial discretion regarding the determination of damages and entitlement to attorneys' fees and other costs;

9. May, in the absence of a waiver or consent, discharge a guarantor to the extent that (a) action by a creditor impairs the value of collateral securing guaranteed debt to the detriment of the guarantor, or (b) guaranteed debt is materially modified;

10. May permit a party who has materially failed to render or offer performance required by the contract to cure that failure unless (a) permitting a cure would unreasonably hinder the aggrieved party from making substitute arrangements for performance, or (b) it was important in the circumstances to the aggrieved party that performance occur by the date stated in the contract;

11. Limit or affect the enforceability of a waiver of a right of redemption;

12. Impose limitations on attorneys' or trustee's fees;

13. Limit or affect the enforceability of any provision that purports to prevent any party from becoming a mortgagee in possession notwithstanding enforcement actions taken under the Loan Documents; and

14. Limit or affect the enforceability of provisions for late charges, prepayment charges, or yield maintenance charges, and acceleration of future amounts due (other than principal) without appropriate discount to present value, liquidated damages, late charges, prepayment charges and increased interest rates upon default, and other "penalties"; provided, however, that the qualification contained in this Section H.14 shall not limit our opinions set forth in Section D.18 or Section D.19 above.

I. **Additional Qualifications — California.**

We express no opinion as to the validity or enforceability of any provisions of the Loan Documents that:

1. Require a borrower to provide hazard insurance coverage against risks in an amount exceeding the replacement value of any improvements to real property;

2. Impose requirements respecting impound accounts in conflict with applicable law;

3. Provide for the application of insurance or condemnation proceeds to reduce indebtedness;

4. Purport to make any assignment of rents, issues, and profits from the Deed of Trust Collateral enforceable without the lender taking steps to enforce in accordance with applicable law or which purport to allow the lender to collect rents, issues, and profits and not apply those collections to the indebtedness secured by the Loan Documents;

5. Contain a waiver of any party's statutory right to reinstate a secured obligation by paying the delinquent amounts of the fully accelerated debt at any time prior to the time provided by statute or that contain a waiver of any right of redemption;

6. Are in conflict with any laws governing foreclosure and disposition procedures regarding any collateral or in conflict with any limitations on attorneys' or trustees' fees;

7. Indemnifies any party against its own negligence or willful misconduct;

8. Are in conflict with the real property antideficiency, fair value, security first, and one form of action provisions of California law;

9. Provide for the acceleration of any indebtedness upon any transfer or further encumbrance of any of the collateral for any loan, or upon a change of ownership of any entity which directly or indirectly owns any interest in any such collateral, except to the extent that (a) such provisions are made enforceable pursuant to the federal preemption afforded by the Garn–St. Germain Depository Institutions Act of 1982, as set forth at 12 U.S.C. 1701j-3 and the regulations adopted pursuant thereto or (b) enforcement is reasonably necessary to protect against impairment of the lender's security or an increase in the risk of default;

10. [intentionally omitted];

11. Provide that time is of the essence;

12. Provide for the confession of judgment;

13. Contain a waiver of (i) broadly or vaguely stated rights; (ii) the benefits of statutory, regulatory, or constitutional rights, unless and to the extent the statute, regulation, or constitution explicitly allows waiver; (iii) unknown future defenses; and (iv) rights to damages;

14. Attempt to change or waive rules of evidence or fix the method or quantum of proof to be applied in litigation or similar proceedings;

15. Select the forum for the resolution of any disputes or consent to the jurisdiction of any jurisdiction (both as to personal jurisdiction and subject matter jurisdiction); or

16. Appoint one party as an attorney-in-fact for an adverse party.

With respect to the opinions and qualifications set forth herein, you should be aware of the following provisions of California law:

> a. Section 726 of the California Code of Civil Procedure provides that any action to recover on a debt or other right secured by a mortgage or a deed of trust on real property must comply with the requirements of that section, which requirements relate to and specify the procedures for the sale of encumbered property, the application of proceeds, the rendition in certain cases of a deficiency judgment, and other related matters. We advise you that in such an action or proceeding, the debtor may require the creditor to exhaust all of its security before a personal judgment may be obtained against the debtor for a deficiency. We also advise you that failure to comply with the provisions of Section 726 (including an attempt to exercise a right to set off with

respect to any funds of Borrower that may be deposited with you from time to time and with respect to which you do not hold a perfected security interest) may result in loss of your lien on the real property collateral. *See, e.g., Walker Community Bank*, 10 Cal. 3d 729, 111 Cal. Rptr. 897, 518 P.2d 329 (1974); *Security Pacific National Bank v. Wozab*, 51 Cal. 3d 991, 275 Cal. Rptr. 201, 800 P.2d 557 (1990). For example, in *Security Pacific National Bank v. Wozab, supra*, the lender was held to have lost its lien on real property security by exercising a right of setoff with respect to funds of the borrower deposited with the lender and as to which the lender did not have a security interest.

b. Section 580b of the California Code of Civil Procedure pro-vides that no deficiency judgment shall be rendered upon a purchase-money obligation in favor of the vendor arising from the sale of real property where such purchase-money obligation is secured by a lien on the real property pur-chased from the vendor, or in favor of a lender where the proceeds of the loan are used to purchase a one- to four-family dwelling occupied entirely or in part by the borrower and where such loan is secured by a lien on such dwelling.

c. Section 580d of the California Code of Civil Procedure provides that no deficiency judgment shall be rendered upon a note secured by a deed of trust or mortgage on real property after sale of the real property under the power of sale contained in such deed of trust or mortgage.

d. Section 2924c of the California Civil Code provides that whenever the maturity of an obligation secured by a deed of trust or mortgage on real property is accelerated by rea-son of a default in the payment of interest or in the payment of any installment of principal or other sums secured thereby, or by reason of failure of the trustor or mortgagor to pay taxes, assessments, or insurance premiums, the trustor or mortgagor and certain other specified persons have the right, to be exercised at any time within the rein-statement period described in such section, to cure such default by paying the entire amount then due (including certain reasonable costs and expenses incurred in enforc-ing such obligations but excluding any principal amount that would not then be due had no default occurred) and thereby cure the default and reinstate such deed of trust or mortgage and the obligations secured thereby to the same effect as if no acceleration has occurred. If the power of sale in the deed of trust or mortgage is not to be exercised, such reinstatement right may be exercised at any time prior to entry of the decree of foreclosure.

e. Section 2938 of the California Civil Code deals with the creation, perfection, and enforcement of an assignment of any interest in leases, rents, issues, or profits made in connection with an obligation secured by real property and provides specific provisions regarding the enforcement of such an assignment. We note that the statute has not yet been interpreted judicially. We also note that the only method that is clearly established under California law for enforcement of an assignment of rents is by appointment of a receiver by a court in an action for specific performance of the provisions of the Financing Documents that provide for an assignment of rents.

f. Section 725.5 of the California Code of Civil Procedure authorizes, under certain limited circumstances, a real estate–secured commercial lender to waive its lien against a parcel of "environmentally impaired" security (as therein defined) and sue the borrower without foreclosing on the real property collateral for the loan.

g. Section 736 of the California Code of Civil Procedure permits a lender, under certain limited circumstances, to sue for breach of contract relating to any "environmental provisions" (as therein defined) concerning real property security without foreclosing on the real property security or in an action brought following foreclosure, whether judicial or non-judicial.

h. Sections 580a and 726 of the California Code of Civil Procedure impose fair value limitations on the amount of the deficiency judgment that can be recovered following the foreclosure.

i. Sections 2889 and 2903 through 2905 of the California Civil Code and Sections 729.010 through 729.090 of the California Code of Civil Procedure grant certain redemption rights to persons having an interest in property subject to a lien and prevent the parties to the contract from restraining the right of redemption from a lien.

j. The provisions of Sections 564 *et seq.* of the California Code of Civil Procedure prescribe the manner and circumstances under which appointments of receivers are authorized.

k. California Code of Civil Procedure Section 631(d) provides that a court may, in its discretion upon just terms, allow a trial by jury although there may have been a waiver of trial by jury.

l.   Section 2954.5 of the California Civil Code imposes, among other things, certain notice requirements as a condition precedent to the right of a real property secured lender to assess a default, delinquency, or late payment charge on a delinquent loan payment.

m.   Section 2954.1 of the California Civil Code provides, among other things, that a lender who maintains an impound account for the payment of taxes and assessments on real property, insurance premiums, or other purposes related to such property shall not (i) require the borrower to deposit in such an account in any month an amount in excess of that which would be permitted under the statute, or (ii) require the sums maintained in such account to exceed at any time the amount or amounts reasonably necessary to pay such obligations as they become due.

n.   Section 2955(a) of the California Civil Code provides, among other things, that, subject to the exceptions set forth in California Civil Code Section 2955(b), money held by a beneficiary of a deed of trust on California real property in an impound account for the payment of taxes or assessments or insurance premiums or other purposes on or relating to the property shall be retained in California and, if invested, shall be invested only with residents of California or with entities engaged in business within California. We assume for purposes of this opinion, with Lender's permission, that (one) Lender is a bank, bank subsidiary, bank holding company, or subsidiary of a bank holding company doing business under the authority of and in accordance with the laws of the United States or the State of New York relating to banks, as evidenced by a license, certificate, or charter issued by the United States or the State of New York, (two) the Deed of Trust will constitute, upon due recordation, a first lien on the Property, and (three) any such impound account will be held in a depository institution insured by the Federal Deposit Insurance Corporation, and that accordingly Lender is exempt from the restrictions of Section 2955(a).

o.   The right of Lender under the Loan Documents to apply proceeds collected under fire or other property insurance policies or to apply awards or damages in condemnation proceedings against the secured indebtedness may be subject to a limitation (including, without limitation, under Section 1265.225 of the California Code of Civil Procedure) upon such application where and to the extent that the security under the Loan Documents is not impaired. This limitation does not affect or limit the right of Lender to apply such proceeds to the repair of the encumbered property in accordance with the provisions of the Loan Documents or to receive and control disbursement of such proceeds.

p.   Section 1670.5 of the California Civil Code allows a court to refuse to enforce all or part of any contract or clause in a contract which, as a matter of law, is found to have been unconscionable at the time made or contrary to public policy.

q.   Section 882.020 of the California Civil Code provides that unless the lien of a mortgage, deed of trust, or other instrument that creates a security interest of record in real property to secure a debt or other obligation has earlier expired on the date provided by California Civil Code Section 2911 (*i.e.*, the last day upon which an action can be brought upon the principal obligation), the lien expires at, and is not enforceable by action for foreclosure commenced, power of sale exercised, or any other means asserted after, the later of the following times: (i) if the final maturity date or the last date fixed for payment of the debt or performance of the obligation is ascertainable from the record, 10 years after that date; (ii) if the final maturity date or the last date fixed for payment of the debt or performance of the obligation is not ascertainable from the record, or if there is no final maturity date or last date fixed for payment of the debt or performance of the obligation, 60 years after the date the instrument that created the security interest was recorded; and (iii) if a notice of intent to preserve the security interest is recorded within the time prescribed in clause (i) or (ii) above, 10 years after the date the notice is recorded.

r.   To the extent that the Loan Documents provide for the payment of attorneys' fees in litigation, Section 1717 of the California Civil Code regarding the requirement that such attorneys' fees be reasonable and providing that such provisions extend to both parties to the litigation, whether or not by their express terms they benefit only one party.

J. **Additional Qualifications—Perfection of Security Interests Under the UCC.**

With respect to the perfection of security interests in the UCC Collateral under the UCC and the perfection of security interests in the collateral described in the RC Financing Statements ("RC Collateral"), you should also be aware of, and our opinions are subject to and limited by, the following provisions:

1. We express no opinion as to the perfection of any security interest in any portion of the UCC Collateral or the RC Collateral that is not governed by, or that is excluded from, or which is not perfected by the filing of a financing statement under the Division 9 of the UCC.

2. We have assumed that the debtor has "rights" in the UCC Collateral and the RC Collateral and that "value" has been given, as contemplated by Section 9203 of the UCC.

3. We have assumed that none of the UCC Collateral or the RC Collateral consists of consumer goods or is subject to a statute or treaty of the United States which provides for or which specifies a place of filing different from that specified in the UCC for the filing of the security interest, or any other items excluded from the coverage of the UCC by Section 9104 thereof.

4. We call to your attention the fact that the perfection of a security interest in "Proceeds" (as defined in the UCC) of collateral is governed and restricted by Section 9306 of the UCC.

5. We have assumed that the security interests in any portion of the collateral constituting the "inventory of a retail merchant" (within the meaning of Section 9102 of the UCC) secures a debt as to which the secured party has made no restriction as to use of funds, other than those which are commercially reasonable and made in good faith, as contemplated by Section 9102(5)(b) of the UCC.

6. We note that the law is not well developed with respect to the specificity of description necessary to create a valid security interest in personal property. We express no opinion as to whether the phrase "all property" or similarly general phrases would be held to describe any particular item or items of collateral.

7. In the case of any portion of the UCC Collateral or RC Collateral which becomes subject to a security interest after the date hereof, Section 552 of the Federal Bankruptcy Code limits the extent to which property acquired by a debtor after the commencement of a case under the Federal Bankruptcy Code may be subject to a security interest arising from a security agreement entered into by the debtor before the commencement of such a case.

8. The perfection of any such security interest will be terminated as to any portion of the UCC Collateral or RC Collateral acquired by the Borrower more than four months after the Borrower so changes its name, identity, or corporate structure so as to make the Financing Statements misleading, unless new, appropriate financing statements indicating the new name, identity, or corporate structure of the Borrower are properly filed before the expiration of such four months.

9. We express no opinion as to the validity, binding effect, or enforceability of any provision in the Loan Documents that purports (i) to

permit any person or entity to sell or otherwise dispose of, or purchase, any property or collateral subject thereto, or enforce any other right or remedy thereunder (including, without limitation, any self-help or taking possession remedy), except in compliance with the UCC and other applicable laws; (ii) to limit the ability of any debtor or any other person or entity to transfer voluntarily or involuntarily (by way of sale, creation of a security interest, attachment, levy, garnishment, or other judicial process) its right, title, or interest in or to any collateral subject thereto, as contemplated by Section 9-311 of the UCC; or (iii) to establish standards for the performance of the obligations of good faith, diligence, reasonableness, and care prescribed by the UCC.

10. We express no opinion with respect to the enforceability of the security interests under the Loan Documents to the extent the security interests are in collateral that is acquired after the date of this letter and involve circumstances in which such security interests are deemed to be taken as security for an antecedent debt and other than for new value under Section 9108 of the UCC.

11. The effect of the provisions of the UCC that require a secured party, in any disposition of personal property collateral, to act in good faith and in a commercially reasonable manner.

12. We call to your attention that under the UCC, events occurring subsequent to the date hereof may affect any security interests subject to the UCC and one or more of the following severally applicable provisions may affect the security interest of the Lender including, but not limited to, factors of the type identified in Section 9-306 with respect to proceeds; Section 9-103 with respect to changes in the location of the collateral and the location of the debtor; Section 9-316 with respect to subordination agreements; Section 9-403 with respect to continuation statements; and Sections 9-307, 9-308, and 9-309 with respect to subsequent purchasers of the collateral. In addition, actions taken by a secured party (e.g., releasing or assigning the security interest, delivering possession of the collateral to the debtor or another person, and voluntarily subordinating a security interest) may affect the validity, perfection, or priority of a security interest.

13. In the case of any instrument, chattel paper, account, or general intangible which is itself secured by other property, we express no opinion with respect to the Lender's rights in and to such underlying property.

14. We call to your attention that the American Law Institute and the National Conference of Commissioners on Uniform State Law have approved a revised version of Article 9, with conforming amendments to Articles 1, 2, 2a, 4, 5, 6, 7, and 8, of the Uniform Commercial Code ("Revised Article 9"), which substantially changes the law governing the creation and perfection of security interests. Revised Article 9 has been adopted in California and New York legislatures and will become effective on July 1, 2001. The opinions set forth herein are based solely on the law in effect on the date hereof; accordingly, we express no opinion as to the effect

of Revised Article 9 on the validity, perfection, or priority of the security interest.

K. **Additional Qualifications — Guaranty and Suretyship.**

1. We advise you that, under certain circumstances, a guaranty executed by (i) a general partner (including a general partner through one or more intermediate partnerships) of a partnership borrower or (ii) a shareholder of a corporate principal obligor may not be enforceable as an obligation separate and distinct from the guaranteed obligations described therein if it is determined that the borrower is merely an <u>alter ego</u> or nominee of the guarantor and that the "true" borrower is the guarantor. *See, e.g., Riddle v. Lushing,* 203 Cal. App. 2d 831 (1962); *Valinda Builders v. Vissner,* 230 Cal. App. 2d 106 (1964). This is the case even if the loan is non-recourse to the borrower. *Westinghouse Credit Corp. v. Barton,* 789 F. Supp. 1043 (C.D. Cal. 1992). If a guarantor is deemed to be liable as a principal, and, notwithstanding our opinion regarding the parties' choice of New York law, California law is held to apply to the interpretation and enforcement of the Recourse Guaranty, it is likely that the guarantor will also be entitled to the rights and defenses otherwise available to a principal, including the protection of California's one action and antideficiency laws. For purposes of this opinion, we have assumed, without independent investigation, that neither Borrower nor Recourse Guarantor would be deemed to be the alter ego or nominee of any of the others.

2. We advise you of California statutory provisions and case law to the effect that, in certain circumstances, a guarantor may be exonerated if the creditor materially alters the original obligation of the principal without the consent of the guarantor, elects remedies for default that impair the subrogation rights of the guarantor against the principal, or otherwise takes any action without notifying the guarantor that materially prejudices the guarantor. However, there is authority to the effect that a guarantor may validly waive such rights if the waivers are expressly set forth in the guaranty. *See, e.g., Krueger v. Bank of America,* 145 Cal. App. 3d 204 (1983); Section 2856 of the California Civil Code ("CCC"). Section 2856(b) of the CCC states that any language that expressly sets forth a waiver of the suretyship rights or defenses set forth in Section 2856(a) of the CCC shall be effective, and sets forth specific language which is deemed to create an effective waiver of the guarantor's defense to a recovery by the creditor by reason of the creditor's election of remedies. We note to you, however, a decision of the California Court of Appeal, *Cathay Bank v. Lee,* 14 Cal. App. 4th 1533, 18 Cal. Rptr. 2d 420 (1993), which invalidated certain waivers contained in a guaranty because the Court of Appeal found that the language of the waivers was not sufficiently explicit in informing the guarantor of the nature of the defense purportedly being waived. The reasoning of the *Cathay Bank* opinion could be applied to, and thus could affect, all waivers contained in any Loan Document. We

express no opinion with respect to the effect of (a) any modification to or amendment of the guarantied obligations that materially increases such obligations; (b) any election of remedies by Lender following the occurrence of an event of default; or (c) any other action by Lender that materially prejudices a guarantor, if, in any such instance, such modification, election, or action occurs without the consent of or notice to such guarantor and without granting to such guarantor an opportunity to cure any such default.

L. **Limitations.**

1. We express no opinion with respect to the applicability of the laws of any jurisdiction other than the State of California, the State of New York, the corporate law of the State of Maryland, the Revised Uniform Limited Partnership Act of the State of Delaware, the Limited Liability Company Act of the State of Delaware, and all federal laws, to the extent applicable. Further, this opinion is predicated solely upon laws and regulations in existence as of the present date and as they presently apply and we assume no obligation to advise you of changes that may hereafter be brought to our attention. Without limitation, we express no opinion regarding the laws of the State of Texas.

2. We express no opinion with regard to any laws, statutes, ordinances, rules, or regulations concerning (i) state and federal securities laws, "blue-sky" laws; (ii) the provisions of the Employee Retirement Income Security Act of 1974 or any other state or federal pension or employee benefits laws; (iii) federal and state antitrust laws; (iv) federal and state environmental (except as set forth herein), zoning, health and safety, land use, or subdivision laws; (v) federal and state tax laws and regulations (except for our opinion set forth in Section D.10 regarding mortgage taxes); and (vi) federal and state banking laws.

3. Except as expressly provided in Section D.12 above, we express no opinion as to the perfection of any security interests in any items or types of personal property, and no opinion is expressed with respect to (a) the status or condition of title to any property or (b) the priority of any lien or security interest in any collateral held by or available to Lender with respect to any indebtedness or obligation evidenced by or referenced in the Loan Documents.

4. This opinion is limited to the specific opinions expressed herein, and no further opinions are intended to be, or should be, inferred therefrom. This opinion is given as of the date hereof only, and we expressly decline any undertaking or obligation to supplement this opinion or to advise you (a) if any applicable laws change after the date hereof or (b) if we become aware of any facts or in respect to any transactions occurring subsequent to the date hereof, in any case that might change the opinions expressed herein, in whole or in part.

This opinion is rendered only to Lender and the other addressees in connection with the Loan and the Loan Documents, and only with respect to the Loan and the Loan Documents. This opinion may not be relied upon by any addressee for any other purpose, or relied upon by any other person, firm, or entity for any purpose. The addressees may, however, deliver a copy of this opinion to their respective accountants, attorneys, and other professional advisors; to governmental agencies having jurisdiction over an addressee; to any Loan participants; to any transferees of the addressees; to any party servicing the Loan; and to any rating agency involved in the securitization of the Loan, and any such participants, transferees, servicing agents, and rating agencies may rely on this opinion as if it were addressed and delivered to them on the date hereof. Except as set forth above, this opinion may not be duplicated, paraphrased, quoted, summarized, or reproduced in whole or in part.

Very truly yours,

EXHIBIT A
BORROWER'S CERTIFICATE

EXHIBIT B
SCHEDULE OF SECURITY ACCOUNTS

CHAPTER **10**

BASIC RISK ALLOCATION AND INSURANCE CONCEPTS FOR REAL ESTATE TRANSACTIONS

Aaron Johnston, Jr.
Charles E. Comiskey

§ 10.04   INDEMNITY PROVISIONS

[B]   Components of a Well-Written Indemnity Provision

[9]   Contract Versus Tort

Page 662, Form 10-2, § 1(b), first line, delete "Obligations" *and substitute:*

obligations

Page 662, Form 10-2, § 1(c), first line, delete "and Waiver."

Page 662, Form 10-2, § 1(c), eighth line, delete "0196" *and substitute:*

1001

[C]   Potential Pitfalls

[4]   Limited Response by Insurer

Page 663, sixth line of subsection [4], delete "personal injury," *and substitute:*

and personal

[6]   Limitations Imposed by Insurance Industry

Page 664, replace first full sentence of carryover paragraph with:

Beginning with the 1996 edition of the Commercial General Liability Insurance form CG 0001 published by Insurance Services Office, Inc., the insurance industry began imposing additional limitations with respect to liability incurred by the insured under a contractual indemnity.

Page 664, replace first indented extract with:

1.   We will pay, with respect to any claim we investigate or settle, or any "suit" against an insured we defend:

   a.   All expenses we incur.

   b.   Up to $250 for cost of bail bonds required because of accidents or traffic law violations arising out of the use of any vehicle to which the Bodily Injury Liability Coverage applies. We do not have to furnish these bonds.

   c.   The cost of bonds to release attachments, but only for bond amounts within the applicable limit of insurance. We do not have to furnish these bonds.

   d.   All reasonable expenses incurred by the insured at our request to assist us in the investigation or defense of the claim or "suit", including actual loss of earnings up to $250 a day because of time off from work.

   e.   All costs taxed against the insured in the "suit".

   f.   Prejudgment interest awarded against the insured on that part of the judgment we pay. If we make an offer to pay the applicable limit of insurance, we will not pay any prejudgment interest based on that period of time after the offer.

   g.   All interest on the full amount of any judgment that accrues after entry of the judgment and before we have paid, offered to pay, or deposited in court the part of the judgment that is within the applicable limit of insurance.

   These payments will not reduce the limits of insurance.

[D] Fair Notice Rules (Texas Rules)

[1] Express Negligence Rule

Page 666, add to note 1 after "705":

, 707

Page 666, add to note 2 after "455":

, 459

Page 666, add to note 3 after "813":

, 814

[2] Conspicuous

Page 667, add to note 4 after "505":

, 510

§ 10.05 WAIVER, RELEASE AND EXCULPATION

[B] Fair Notice

Page 668, add at end of note 5:

at 509.

[C] Contracts of Adhesion

Page 668, add to note 6 after "887":

, 889

§ 10.07   LIABILITY INSURANCE

[C]   Basic Concepts

[3]   Editions

Page 673, replace sixth sentence of subsection [3] with:

Numerous editions of the commercial general liability policy have been published since 1986.

[I]   Additional Insured

[2]   Evidence

Page 686, replace "Form 25-S" on first line of page with:

Form 25

Page 686, in last sentence of carryover paragraph, replace "Form 25-S, issued in July 1997," with:

Form 25

[5]   Sample Additional Insured Forms

[a]   *Additional Insured—Owners, Lessees, or Contractors (CG 2010 1093)*

Page 690, replace first sentence of subsection [a] with:

Note that this form covers only ongoing operations and therefore presumably does not cover completed operations.

[6]   "Other Insurance" and Additional Insureds

Page 692, in first line of carryover paragraph, replace "the ISO 1998" with:

an ISO 1998 or later edition of the

§ 10.08   PROPERTY INSURANCE

[A]   Definition

[1]   Basic Coverages

[a]   *Fire and Extended Coverage Insurance*

Page 693, add after second sentence of subsection [a]:

Two types of property insurance policies currently provide some of the coverages formerly known as "fire and extended coverage": causes of loss—basic form, and causes of loss—broad form.

[d]   *Causes of Loss—Special Form*

Page 695, add after (o):

(p) Terrorism and biocontaminants.

[2]   Special Coverages with Respect to Additional Causes of Loss

[a]   *Legal Liability Coverage*

Page 695, add at end of seventh line of extract:

We may investigate and settle any claim or "suit" at our discretion.

[c]   *Boiler/Machinery*

Page 696, add at end of subsection [c]:

If a boiler & machinery policy is provided by a different insurance company from that providing the primary property insurance, the authors recommend adding a Joint or Disputed Loss Agreement (CP 12 72 on the property insurance) to both policies. The Joint or Disputed Loss Agreement requires that the insurance companies jointly pay a covered loss and agree to settle any disputes between themselves as to which policy should apply.

[d] Earthquake

Page 696, replace the last sentence of subsection [d] with:

Coverage can be obtained through ISO form 1040 0899, a difference in conditions policy, or as an endorsement to a property policy.

[3] Special Coverages with Respect to Specific Types of Property

[f] Leasehold Interest

Page 698, replace last sentence of first paragraph before extract with:

ISO form CP 0060 0695 provides, in part, as follows:

[5] Special Coverages with Respect to Party Covered

[b] Loss Payees

Page 703, delete "0695" at end of first line.

[B] Basic Concepts

[1] "Subrogation"

[b] Components of Well-Written Waive of Subrogation

Page 705, add at end of "Comment" in FORM 10-6:

If this form is used in the State of Texas, the second sentence should be in bold print to comply with the Express Negligence Rule.

[c] Availability

Page 705, replace note 8 with:

[8] *International Ins. Co. v. Medical Prof'l Building of Corpus Christi*, 405 S.W.2d 867, 869 (Tex. App. — Corpus Christi 1966).

[2]   "Co-Insurance"

Page 707, in second line of "Example," replace "fire insurance" *with:*

property insurance

[C]   Value of Property Insured

[5]   Debris Removal and Changes in Law

Page 712, replace second sentence of subsection [5] with:

Debris removal is provided as Additional Coverages under a commercial property policy and is limited to 25 percent of the amount paid for the loss plus the deductible. If the entire limit is required to reconstruct the damaged property, a $10,000 additional limit is available for debris removal. Higher limits can be purchased by using Debris Removal Additional Limit of Insurance (CP 04 15).

Page 713, replace entire extract with:

1. Coverage A — Coverage for loss to the Undamaged Portion of the Building

    With respect to the building that has sustained covered direct physical damage, we will pay under Coverage A for the loss in value of the undamaged portion of the building as a consequence of enforcement of an ordinance or law that requires demolition of undamaged parts of the same building.

    Coverage A is included within the Limit of Insurance shown in the Declarations as applicable to the covered building. Coverage A does not increase the Limit of Insurance.

2. Coverage B — Demolition Cost Coverage

    With respect to the building that has sustained covered direct physical damage, we will pay the cost to demolish and clear the site of undamaged parts of the same building, as a consequence of enforcement of an ordinance or law that requires demolition of such undamaged property.

    The Coinsurance Additional Condition does not apply to Demolition Cost Coverage.

3.   Coverage C — Increased Cost of Construction Coverage

a. With respect to the building that has sustained covered direct physical damage, we will pay the increased cost to:

(1)   Repair or reconstruct damaged portions of that building; and/or

(2)   Reconstruct or remodel undamaged portions of that building, whether or not demolition is required;

when the increased cost is a consequence of enforcement of the minimum requirements of the ordinance or law.

However:

(1)   This coverage applies only if the restored or remodeled property is intended for similar occupancy as the current property, unless such occupancy is not permitted by zoning or land use ordinance or law.

(2)   We will not pay for the increased cost of construction if the building is not repaired, reconstructed or remodeled.

The Coinsurance Additional Condition does not apply to Increased Cost of Construction Coverage.

b. When a building is damaged or destroyed and Coverage C applies to that building in accordance with 3.a. above, coverage for the increased cost of construction also applies to repair or reconstruction of the following, subject to the same conditions stated in 3.a.:

(1)   The cost of excavations, grading, backfilling and filling;

(2)   Foundation of the building;

(3)   Pilings; and

(4)   Underground pipes, flues and drains.

The items listed in b.(1) through b.(4) above are deleted from Property Not Covered, but only with respect to the coverage described in this Provision, 3.b.

§ 10.09   QUALITY AND EVIDENCE OF INSURANCE

[C]   Evidencing the Existence of Coverage

[2]   ACORD Form 25-S, "Certificate of Liability Insurance"

Page 716, replace every reference to "Form 25-S" *with* "Form 25."

[a]   Disclaimers

Pages 716-717, replace every reference to "Form 25-S" *with* "Form 25."

Page 716, eighth line of subsection [a], replace "July 1997" *with:*

1998

[b]   Use with Liability Policies

Page 717, replace every reference to "Form 25-S" *with* "Form 25."

§ 10.10   OTHER TERMS COMMONLY ENCOUNTERED

[D]   Problems with Self-Insurance

[1]   Lack of Controlling Law

Page 721, add at end of subsection [1]:

When a deductible is in place, the insurer will defend the policyholder no matter the magnitude of the claim, but, in effect, pays only for the portion of the loss in excess of the amount of the deductible. Depending on the wording of the policy, the deductible can apply on a per occurrence basis or a per claim basis. In the event of multiple claims arising out of one occurrence, a per claim basis could prove catastrophic to the insured party. A deductible sometimes erodes the policy limit.

[2]   Verification of Creditworthiness

Page 721, add at end of subsection [2]:

When a self-insured retention ("SIR") is in place, the insurer will not provide a defense unless the claim exceeds the amount of the SIR and will pay only for the portion of the loss in excess of the amount of the SIR. Depending on the wording of the policy, the SIR can apply on a per occurrence basis or a per claim basis. In the event of multiple claims arising out of one occurrence, a per claim basis could prove catastrophic to the insured party. The full policy limit is usually available in excess of the SIR.

APPENDIX 10B
TENANT'S INSURANCE

Page 725, second column, third row in the table, sixth line, change: "products/completed" *to* "product-completed."

Page 737, add new appendix:

APPENDIX 10G
DEED OF TRUST INSURANCE, INDEMNITY, AND
WAIVER PROVISIONS
(MORTGAGEE'S FORM)

1. **INSURANCE.** For so long as the Indebtedness remains outstanding, Grantor will, at Grantor's sole expense, procure and maintain the following insurance coverages:

    (a) **Property Insurance.**

        (i)   **Form.** "Causes of loss—special form" (formerly known as "all risks"). No exclusions permitted other than standard printed exclusions.

        (ii)   **Limit.** Full replacement cost.

        (iii)   **Coverage.** All improvements constituting a part of the Mortgaged Property and all furniture, fixtures, and equipment located therein.

        (iv)   **Endorsements.**

            (1)   Ordinance of law coverage endorsement;

            (2)   Standard Mortgagee Clause; and

            (3)   Flood insurance if the Mortgaged Property is located in a special flood hazard area, as defined in the Flood Disaster Act of 1973.

        (v)   **Waiver of Subrogation.** In favor of Lender Parties.

    (b) **Business Income Insurance.** [*Loss of rents equivalent coverage if Grantor is leasing all or a portion of the Mortgaged Property to third parties or business interruption equivalent coverage if Grantor is the sole occupant of the Mortgaged Property.*]

        (i)   **Limit.** [*Coverage for no less than 12 months of rents if loss of rents equivalent is required or 6 months of income and expenses if business interruption equivalent is required.*]

        (ii)   **Waiver of Subrogation.** In favor of Lender Parties.

    (c) **Commercial General Liability Insurance ("CGL").**

        (i)   **Form.** ISO CG 0001 1001 or equivalent.

        (ii)   **Basis.** Occurrence.

(iii) **Limits.** $1,000,000 per occurrence

$2,000,000 general aggregate

$2,000,000 product-completed operations aggregate limit

$1,000,000 personal and advertising injury limit

$ 50,000 damage to premises rented to you limit

$ 5,000 medical expense limit

(iv) **Required Endorsements.**

    (1)   Aggregate limits of insurance per location;

    (2)   Lender Parties will be included as "additional insureds" using ISO additional insured form CG 2026 1185, without modification;

    (3)   A waiver of subrogation in favor of Lender Parties;

    (4)   A deletion of the contractual claim exclusions for personal injury and advertising injury; and

    (5)   Severability of interests.

(v) **Other Insurance.** Policy to contain standard CGL "other insurance" wording, unmodified in any way that would make Grantor's coverage excess over or contributory with the additional insured's own commercial general liability coverage.

(vi) **Deductible.** No deductible or self-insured retention in excess of $10,000 to apply to any coverage provided by the CGL policy without the prior written approval of Lender.

(d) **Workers' Compensation and Employer Liability Coverage.**

  (i) **Workers' Compensation.** Statutory limits (if state has no statutory limit, $1,000,000).

  (ii) **Alternative Forms.** No "alternative" form of coverage shall be accepted.

  (iii) **Employer's Liability.** Employer's liability limits: $1,000,000 each accident for bodily injury by accident or $1,000,000 each employee for bodily injury by disease.

  (iv) **Waiver of Subrogation.** In favor of Lender Parties.

(e) **Business Auto Liability Insurance.**

  (i) **Basis.** Occurrence.

  (ii) **Limit.** $1,000,000 per occurrence.

    (iii) **Required Endorsements.**

        (1) Lender Parties will be included as "additional insureds"; and

        (2) A waiver of subrogation in favor of Lender Parties.

(f) **Umbrella Liability Insurance.**

    (i) **Basis.** Occurrence.

    (ii) **Limit.** $5,000,000 per occurrence.

        $ 5,000,000 aggregate

    (iii) **Required Endorsements.**

        (1) Aggregate limits of insurance per location;

        (2) Lender Parties will be included as "additional insureds"; and

        (3) To have same date of inception and expiration as CGL policy.

(g) **Other Grantor Insurance Coverage.** Grantor will, at Grantor's sole expense, procure and maintain any other and further insurance coverages that Lender or Lender's lender may require.

(h) **Form of Policies and Additional Requirements.**

    (i) **Insurance Carrier Requirements.** Bests Rating of "A," or better, and Bests Financial Size Category of VIII, or better, and/or *Standard & Poor Insurance Solvency Review* A–, or better. All carriers admitted to engage in the business of insurance in the State or Commonwealth in which the Mortgaged Property is located.

    (ii) **Other Insurance.** All policies must be endorsed to be primary policies of Lender and lender being excess, secondary, and noncontributing.

    (iii) **Notice.** No cancellation, nonrenewal, or material modification without 30 days' prior written notice by insurance carrier to Lender and lender.

    (iv) **Aggregate Limits.** Lender must be notified in writing immediately by Grantor of claims against Grantor that might cause a reduction below seventy-five percent (75%) of any aggregate limit of any policy.

    (v) **Evidence of Grantor's Insurance.**

        (1) Property and business income insurance must be evidenced by ACORD form 27, "Evidence of Property Insurance."

(2) CGL and workers' compensation insurance must be evidenced by ACORD form 25s, "Certificate of Liability Insurance."

(3) Certificate or evidence of insurance must be delivered together with executed Deed of Trust and a new certificate or evidence of insurance must be delivered no later than 30 days prior to expiration of existing policy.

(vi) **Endorsements.** Copies of endorsements must be attached to ACORD forms 25s and 27 delivered to Lender. "Additional insured" or "beneficiary" on endorsements should be "Lender Parties" as defined in Paragraph 2(a) of this Deed of Trust.

2. **INDEMNITIES AND WAIVERS.**

(a) **Definitions.** For purposes of this Deed of Trust:

(i) **Grantor Parties.** "Grantor Parties" means (A) Grantor and (B) Grantor's shareholders, members, partners, directors, officers, employees, sublessees, licensees, invitees, agents, and contractors;

(ii) **Lender Parties.** "Lender Parties" means (A) Lender, (B) Trustee, (C) shareholders, members, partners, affiliates, and subsidiaries, and (D) any directors, officers, employees, agents, or contractors of such persons or entities;

(iii) **Indemnify.** "Indemnify" means to protect another party against a Liability and/or to compensate a party for a Liability actually incurred;

(iv) **Defend.** "Defend" means to oppose a potential or actual Liability on behalf of another party in litigation or other proceeding with counsel reasonably acceptable to Lender and to pay all costs associated with the preparation or prosecution of the defense;

(v) **Waive.** "Waive" means to knowingly and voluntarily relinquish a right and/or release another party from liability in connection with a claim;

(vi) **Liabilities.** "Liabilities" means all liabilities, claims, damages (including consequential damages), losses, penalties, litigation, demands, causes of action (whether in tort or contract, in law or at equity or otherwise), suits, proceedings, judgments, disbursements, charges, assessments, and expenses (including attorneys' and experts' fees and expenses incurred in investigating, defending, or prosecuting any litigation, claim, or proceeding);

(vii) **ISO.** The term "ISO" means Insurance Services Office;

(viii) **Personal Injury, Bodily Injury, and Mortgaged Property Damage.** "Bodily Injury," "Personal Injury," "Mortgaged Property Damage," and "Advertising Injury" will have the same meanings as in the form of commercial general insurance policy CG 0001 1001 issued by ISO. The definitions will not be limited by any exclusions contained in such form; and

(ix) **Grantor's Insurable Injuries.** A "Grantor's Insurable Injury" refers to any of the following:

  (1) **Occurrences in the Mortgaged Property.** Any Personal Injury, Bodily Injury, Property Damage, or Advertising Injury whatsoever occurring in the Mortgaged Property;

  (2) **Occurrences Outside the Mortgaged Property.** Any Personal Injury, Bodily Injury, or Advertising Injury caused by a Grantor Party and occurring outside the Mortgaged Property; or

  (3) **Property Damage.** Any Mortgaged Property Damage suffered by a Grantor Party on the Mortgaged Property.

(b) **Indemnities with Respect to Performance.** To the fullest extent permitted by law, Grantor will Indemnify and Defend Lender Parties against all Liabilities arising out of the following:

  (i) **Conduct of Business.** The conduct of Grantor's business;

  (ii) **Violation of Applicable Law.** The violation of or failure to comply with, or the alleged violation of or alleged failure to comply with, any Applicable Law by a Grantor Party;

  (iii) **Breach of Deed of Trust.** Any breach, violation, or non-performance of any term, condition, covenant, or other obligation of Grantor under this Deed of Trust or any other Loan Document; or

  (iv) **Misrepresentations.** Any misrepresentations made by Grantor or any guarantor of Grantor's obligations in connection with this Deed of Trust or any other Loan Document.

(c) **Indemnities with Respect to Grantor's Insurable Injuries.** To the fullest extent permitted by law, Grantor will Indemnify and Defend Lender Parties against Liabilities arising from Grantor's Insurable Injuries.

(d) **Waiver.** To the fullest extent permitted by law, Grantor, on behalf of all Grantor Parties, Waives all Liabilities against Lender Parties arising from Insurable Risks.

(e) **<u>Scope of Indemnities and Waivers</u>.** The Indemnities, Waivers, and obligations to Defend contained in this Deed of Trust (i) *will be enforced even if the Liability in question is caused by the active or passive negligence or sole, joint, concurrent, or comparative negligence of any of the Lender Parties, and regardless of whether liability without fault or strict liability is imposed or sought to be imposed on any of the Lender Parties, but not to the extent of the percentage of Liabilities that a final judgment of a court of competent jurisdiction establishes under the comparative negligence principles of the State or Commonwealth in which the Mortgaged Property is located, that a Liability was proximately caused by the willful misconduct or gross negligence of that Lender Party (provided, however, that in such event the Indemnity or Waiver will remain valid for all other Lender Parties)*, (ii) are independent of, and will not be limited by, each other or any insurance obligations in this Deed of Trust (whether or not complied with), and (iii) will survive the expiration or earlier termination of this Deed of Trust until all Liabilities against Lender Parties are fully and finally barred by the applicable statutes of limitations.

CHAPTER 11
ENVIRONMENTAL ISSUES IN COMMERCIAL REAL ESTATE SALES AND LEASES
Jack Fersko*

§ 11.02   LAWS IMPOSING ENVIRONMENTAL LIABILITY— GENERALLY

[C]   Common Law

Page 743, add to note 5:

See also Z.A.O., Inc. v. Yarbrough Drive Ctr. Joint Venture, 50 S.W.3d 531 (Tex. Ct. App. 2001). Although the Texas Court of Appeals upheld a breach of contract claim under a lease due to contamination of a gas station site by a former tenant, the court determined that an action in trespass cannot be supported when the contaminants existing do not exceed state action levels, and that a nuisance claim cannot be upheld when the proofs do not establish that the discharge was the result of a negligent or intentional encroachment upon the interest of another.

See also Adams v. Cleveland-Cliffs Iron Co., 237 Mich. App. 51, 67, 602 N.W.2d 215, 222 (1999). In a case of first impression for the Michigan courts, the Court of Appeals of Michigan distinguished between trespass and nuisance, holding that to prevail in trespass, a plaintiff must prove an "intrusion of a physical, tangible object" that is not supported by vibrations, noise, dust, and smoke emanating from the defendant's mining operations. Rather, such intangible intrusions would support only a nuisance claim, provided the plaintiff establishes the intrusions were unreasonable and resulted in significant harm.

---

* The author gratefully acknowledges the assistance of Julie Demaree, an associate of Farer Fersko, a Professional Association, and Michael T. Young, a summer associate of the firm, in the preparation of this 2004 Cumulative Supplement.

§ 11.03 THE COMPREHENSIVE ENVIRONMENTAL RESPONSE, COMPENSATION, AND LIABILITY ACT

Page 743, add to note 6:

See generally Commander Oil Corp. v. Barlo Equip. Corp., 215 F.3d 321 (2d Cir. 2000), *cert. denied*, 121 S. Ct. 427, 148 L. Ed. 2d 436 (2000). In a case of first impression before the U.S. Court of Appeals for the Second Circuit, the court faced the issue of whether a lessee/sublessor could be held liable as an "owner" under CERCLA. Although the court determined that "owner" liability should not attach in the matter *sub judice*, the court did conclude that there may, in fact, be circumstances in which "owner" liability should attach to a lessee. In reaching this conclusion, the court pointed to a number of factors that could transform a tenant into an owner for purposes of CERCLA, including (1) the lease term; (2) control over space use; (3) the landlord's inability to terminate a lease prior to the expiration of the lease term; (4) the lessee's right to sublease; (5) the lessee's responsibility for the payment of taxes, insurance, and maintenance costs; and (6) the lessee's responsibility for structural repairs. It is therefore important for a tenant under a long-term lease or a "bond" lease to consider the implications of potential "owner" liability under CERCLA.

Page 745, add to note 18:

See Container Group Inc. v. American Financial Group, Inc., 128 F. Supp. 2d 470 (S.D. Ohio 2001) wherein the court held that a party will lose the "innocent landowner defense" if such party does not establish that they exercised due care concerning the hazardous substance at issue; *Thomson Precision Ball Co. LLC v. PSB Assocs. Liquidating Trust*, 2001 U.S. Dist. LEXIS 340 (D. Conn. 2001) (order denying renewed motion to dismiss). In *Thomson*, the U.S. District Court for the District of Connecticut held that a purchaser of real estate can achieve innocent landowner status even when the purchaser acquires property knowing of contamination. If the purchaser can establish that it did not know or have reason to know of the hazardous substances complained of in the suit, the purchaser is entitled to "partial" innocent landowner status.

Pages 745–746, delete from last sentence of last full paragraph, beginning with "In determining what constitutes good ..." to end of section, and replace with:

On January 11, 2002, the Brownfields Revitalization and Environmental Restoration Act (Brownfields Act) — was signed into law. The Brownfields Act clarified the innocent landowner defense to CERCLA by defining the pre-acquisition due diligence criteria that must be satisfied in order to benefit from the innocent landowner defense to CERCLA liability.

Specifically, the Brownfields Act sets forth two interim, but specific pre-acquisition criteria. First, for non-residential property, or residential property purchased by a commercial entity, the "all appropriate inquiries" requirement can be satisfied by compliance with the procedures set forth in the ASTM Standard Practice E 1527-97, entitled "Standard Practice for Environmental Site Assessment: Phase 1 Environmental Site Assessment Process."

Second, for the purchase of residential property by a non-governmental or non-commercial entity, "all appropriate inquiries" means an inspection and title search that reveals no basis for further investigation. The Brownfields Act requires the EPA to promulgate permanent standards by January 2004. The permanent standards have been drafted by the Negotiated Rulemaking Committee on All Appropriate Inquiry, consisting of representatives of various interest groups.

On May 9, 2003, the EPA issued a rule titled "Clarification to Interim Standards and Practices for All Appropriate Inquiry Under CERCLA" that was effective on June 9, 2003, and was published in the Federal Register, Volume 68, Number 90 at page 24888 *et seq*. This rule is an interim rule, effective pending the EPA's promulgation of a permanent standard pursuant to the requirements of the Brownfields Act. The rule clarifies that the "all appropriate inquiries" can be satisfied by employing the 1997 ASTM standard for site assessment referred to above, or by following the more current version, referred to as the ASTM E 1527–00 standard.

In the event that hazardous substances are subsequently discovered at the real property, the property owner must exercise appropriate care by taking reasonable steps to prevent and stop any release, and to prevent or limit human, environmental, or natural resource exposure to any previously released hazardous substance. However, the Brownfields Act does not require the innocent landowner to investigate or cleanup the release of hazardous substances.

On November 14, 2003, the Negotiated Rulemaking Committee on All Appropriate Inquiry adopted a draft regulation entitled, "Proposed Standard for Environmental Due Diligence to Avoid Superfund Liability," which will be used by the EPA as the new regulation for satisfying the "all appropriate inquiries" requirement of CERCLA, replacing the ASTM guidance. The EPA is in the process of preparing the general materials to be published along with the proposed rule so that the standard can become a final rule of the EPA.

Based upon the directives of the Brownfields Act, the draft regulation provides that "all appropriate inquiries" under CERCLA § 105(35)(B) must include the results of an inquiry conducted by an environmental professional which takes into account:

1. interviews provided by past and present owners, operators, and occupants;

2. evaluations of historical sources of information;

3. searches for recorded environmental cleanup liens;

4. analysis of federal, tribal, state, and local government records; and

5. visual inspections of the facility and of adjoining properties;

6. the degree of the obviousness of the contamination and the ability to detect the contamination by appropriate investigation; and

7. commonly known or reasonably ascertainable information about the property.

These criteria are quoted in the *Proposed Standard for Environmental Due Diligence to Avoid Superfund Liability*, adopted November 14, 2003, by Negotiated Rulemaking Committee, Env't Rep. (BNA) No. 47, at 2620 (Nov. 23, 2003).

The proposed regulation clarifies at each step what actions are necessary to satisfy the standards and procedures set forth above. In addition, persons seeking to invoke a CERCLA liability defense must reveal to an environmental professional any particularized knowledge or experience concerning the subject property and the surrounding areas, the correlation between the purchase price of the subject property and the fair market value if the property was not contaminated, and any other information that is either generally known or reasonably discoverable.

The new regulation specifically requires the hiring of an environmental professional, which is defined to mean a person who meets specific education and experience requirements necessary to render a professional judgment. The environmental professional must develop opinions and conclusions about releases or threatened releases of hazardous substances concerning the subject property sufficient to satisfy certain objective and performance standards. In carrying out his/her duties, an environmental professional must conduct an environmental site assessment following the standards and practices discussed above. Among other things, the inquiry should seek to reveal present and historical uses of hazardous substances at the subject property and neighboring and adjoining properties, potentially harmful waste management and disposal practices, and the presence of engineering and institutional controls. As an additional requirement, persons performing site characterization and assessments pursuant to a Brownfields grant must inquire into current and past uses of the subject property and past corrective actions associated with petroleum and petroleum products.

In gathering information about the property, the environmental professional's inquiry must include interviews with past and present owners, operators, and occupants of the facility. The inquiry may also include interviews of current and past facility managers who can provide relevant information as to the past uses and physical characteristics of the property as well as their employees. The regulation provides that in situations involving specifically defined "abandoned" sites where the current owner is unavailable for interview and where evidence of potential unauthorized uses or access to the subject property exists, an environmental professional's inquiry must include an interview of at least one owner or occupant of a neighboring or nearby property who can provide relevant information.

In addition, environmental professionals must review historical records and information concerning the site to determine previous uses and occupancies of the property and to identify past and ongoing activities that could have contributed to or resulted in a hazardous release. Documents such as fire insurance maps, chain of title documents, and land use maps may satisfy this search. The review must date back to when the property was first developed for agrarian, residential, commercial, or governmental uses. The regulation, however, provides for some leeway by permitting an environmental professional to rely on professional judgment as to how far back in time it is necessary to search historical records to trace past uses of the property.

The environmental professional also must review federal, state, and local government records to determine whether any activities could have resulted in a hazardous release impacting the site. This review includes searching for records and databases pertaining to nearby and adjoining properties as well as records concerning the subject property. The search distance for which records must be obtained from the subject property boundary is clarified by the regulation. Although the regulation defines specific parameters for various recorded conditions, it also provides that the search distance may be modified by the judgment of an environmental professional to account for such factors as development densities and geologic conditions.

The environmental professional must also conduct a visual onsite inspection of the site. However, in unusual circumstances where such an inspection is impossible because of physical limitations, geographic impediments, or other obstacles to access, an environmental professional may inspect the property by other means. It is important to note that the refusal of a voluntary seller to permit access is not considered an unusual circumstance under the regulation. The regulation provides that in the unusual circumstance in which an inspection is not possible, the requirement may be satisfied through alternative methods such as aerial imagery. In such circumstance, the environmental professional's inquiry must include documentation of efforts to obtain access and documentation of other information consulted to determine the existence of releases or threatened releases.

[A]   Bona Fide Prospective Purchaser Defense*

When Congress created the innocent landowner defense to CERCLA liability in 1986, that defense was only available to property owners who did not know and had no reason to know of the presence of hazardous substances when the property was acquired. Therefore, the defense did not protect a buyer who knew, prior to acquisition, that the property was contaminated.

The Brownfields Act extends the innocent landowner defense to the acquisition of contaminated property by a "bona fide prospective purchaser." A bona fide prospective purchaser is defined to mean a person (or that person's tenant) who acquired ownership of a contaminated property after the enactment of the Brownfields Act, who is able to establish the following by a preponderance of the evidence:

1. The property was contaminated before the new owner acquired it and, before acquiring the property, the new owner made "all appropriate inquiries" into the previous ownership and uses of the property in accordance with generally accepted good commercial and

---

*Portions of this section were adapted from an article by the author presented in *ACREL News*, Vol. 20, No. 3 (Dec. 2002).

customary standards and practices, meaning, in compliance with the ASTM criteria referred to above; although once the EPA promulgates its final regulation on the "all appropriate inquiries" standard, then that will be the criteria to be followed.

2. The new owner provided all legally required notices with respect to the discovery or release of hazardous substances at the property, and complied with any request for information issued by the EPA under CERCLA.

3. The new owner provided full cooperation, assistance, and access to any party that is authorized to conduct a response action or natural resource restoration at the property, complied with any land use restrictions related to the response action, and did not impede the effectiveness of any institutional control.

4. The new owner is not potentially liable, or affiliated with any other entity that is potentially liable for the response costs at the property.

In a case of first impression for the U.S. Court of Appeals for the Ninth Circuit, the court in *Carson Harbor Village, Ltd. v. Unocal Corp.*, 270 F.3d 863 (9th Cir. 2001), *cert. denied*, 2002 U.S. LEXIS 2176, 70 U.S.L.W. 3614 (Apr. 1, 2002), ruled after a rehearing en banc, that the migration of contamination on property does not constitute "disposal" under CERCLA. (In contrast, the court in *Castaic Lake Water Agency v. Whittaker Corp.*, 272 F. Supp. 2d 1053 (C.D. Cal. 2003), held that passive migration, while not a "disposal," constitutes "leaching," thereby placing passive migration within CERCLA's definition of "release" exposing this type of activity to potential liability).

This case involved a claim by a current property owner, Carson Harbor Village, Ltd. (Carson Harbor), for reimbursement, in part, from a predecessor in title for environmental cleanup costs incurred by Carson Harbor. Carson Harbor is the owner and operator of a mobile home park in California. Its predecessor in title, Carson Harbor Village Mobile Home Park, a general partnership (the Partnership), owned and operated the site from 1977 until 1983. The Partnership also operated the site as a mobile home park. Prior to the Partnership's ownership, the property was operated by Unocal Corporation, which leased the site and engaged in petroleum production at the site. Wetlands comprised approximately 17 acres of the site.

During an attempt by Carson Harbor to refinance the property, the lender performed an environmental investigation of the site and discovered "tar-like and slag materials in the wetlands area of the property." Further due diligence revealed that the "materials were a waste or by-product of petroleum production and that they had been on the property for several decades prior to its development as a mobile home park."

Carson Harbor filed suit to recover its cleanup costs advancing a number of theories for relief, including a claim for contribution under CERCLA. The district court granted the Partnership summary judgment, holding, in part, that the Partnership was not a potentially responsible party under CERCLA "because 'disposal warranting CERCLA liability requires a showing that hazardous substances were affirmatively introduced into the environment.'" On appeal, a three-judge panel held that the former property owner may be liable under CERCLA for the passive migration of contamination occurring during its period of ownership. On rehearing, the court held that "passive migration of contaminants through soil during ... ownership" is not "disposal" within the plain meaning of CERCLA. In doing so, the court positioned itself with the Second, Third, and Sixth Circuits, and at odds with the Fourth Circuit. *United States v. CDMG Realty Co.*, 96 F.3d 706 (3d Cir. 1996); *ABB Industrial Sys., Inc. v. Prime Tech. Inc.*, 120 F.3d 351 (2d Cir. 1997); *United States v. 150 Acres of Land*, 104 F.3d 698 (6th Cir. 2000). *See also People v. Thoro Prods. Co., Inc.*, 70 P.3d 1188 (Colo. 2003) (holding that passive migration does not constitute disposal for purposes of a criminal provision of a hazardous waste law). *But see Nurad, Inc. v. William E. Hooper & Sons Co.*, 966 F.2d 837 (4th Cir. 1992).

The court's decision is useful for its precise examination of the subtle differences between the decisions of the other circuit courts, recognizing that "their holdings suggests a more nuanced range of views, depending in large part on the factual circumstances of the case," rather than a clear split concerning the distinction between active versus passive disposal. The court observed that the Fourth Circuit first looked at this issue in the context of a leaking underground storage tank, and rejected the requirement for "'active human conduct.'" Accordingly, the Fourth Circuit in *Nurad, Inc. v. William E. Hopper & Sons Co.*, 966 F.2d 837 (4th Cir. 1992), concluded that the owner of a property at the time of a spill or leak has disposal liability for purposes of CERCLA.

The court also focused on (1) the Third Circuit's decision in *United States v. CDMG Realty Co.*, 96 F.3d 706 (3d Cir. 1996), which concluded "that 'the passive migration of contamination dumped in the land prior to [the past owner's] ownership does not constitute disposal,'" but demurred on deciding "'whether the movement of contaminants unaided by human conduct can ever constitute disposal'"; (2) the Second Circuit's decision in *ABB Indus. Sys., Inc. v. Prime Tech., Inc.*, 120 F.3d 351 (2d Cir. 1997), which followed the Third Circuit's holding and determined that the mere gradual movement of contamination in soil is not disposal, also demurred on the issue of liability of a passive prior property owner of a site with leaking barrels; and (3) the Sixth Circuit's decision in *United States v. 150 Acres of Land*, 204 F.3d 698 (6th Cir. 2000), which determined that in order to have "disposal" there must be "human activity involved in ... [the] movement of hazardous substances ... on the property. ..."

Unfortunately, a writ of certiorari was denied by the United States Supreme Court on April 1, 2002. This is significant for reasons that are more far-reaching than just the disunity within the circuit courts. As discussed above, one of the criteria for qualifying as a bona fide prospective purchaser (BFP) is that a party must establish that disposal of contamination occurred prior to acquisition. However, the ability of a party to satisfy this requirement will now depend upon the jurisdiction in which the property is located. If a property is situated in a jurisdiction that has determined, or in the future does determine, that passive migration is disposal, then BFP status will not be possible. This will undermine the very purpose behind the new federal brownfield law, which is to provide liability protection for developers of contaminated sites and foster re-use of brownfield properties.

For those situated in such a jurisdiction, there was until recently a potential solution in the form of a prospective purchaser agreement with the EPA. The EPA's new Guidance on prospective purchaser agreements, however, reduces significantly the likelihood of now succeeding in consummating such an agreement.

The EPA has negotiated prospective purchaser agreements since 1989, pursuant to which the EPA covenants not to sue a purchaser for the existing contamination on a site. Traditionally, such agreements have been time consuming to negotiate, and have not been liberally entered into by the EPA. On May 31, 2002, EPA issued its Guidance on Prospective Purchaser Agreements in light of the Brownfields Act. According to this new guidance document, the EPA now believes that the Brownfields Act has, for the most part, satisfied the need for a prospective purchaser agreement. Consequently, there are now only a limited set of circumstances when the EPA will consider it necessary to enter into a prospective purchaser agreement.

When a contaminated site is cleaned up, the value of the property will likely be enhanced. Under the Brownfields Act, if the federal government is unable to recover its response costs from third parties, it may impose a "windfall lien" on the real property cleaned up by the federal government. The amount of the lien is not to exceed the increase in the fair market value of the property attributable to the response action. The lien may be satisfied when the bona fide prospective purchaser resells the property. The EPA recognizes in its guidance document that there may be times when a prospective purchaser must resolve in advance of a purchase the extent of the lien, for example, to secure financing. In addition, the EPA recognizes that there may be situations in which there will be substantial public benefits derived from a project that will not otherwise close without a prospective purchaser agreement. Situations referred to in the Guidance include projects that will result in significant environmental benefits, such as where cleanup activity will be undertaken at the site, the facility is the subject of ongoing CERCLA litigation, or serve a significant public interest, and but for the prospective purchaser agreement, the transaction will not otherwise be consummated. Arguably, transactions in jurisdictions that currently treat, or have not yet determined whether, passive migration is a discharge for CERCLA purposes, meets this latter criteria. Because the EPA's new Guidance does make it clear that prospective purchaser agreements will now be subject to greater scrutiny, consideration of a prospective purchaser agreement should be considered early on in a transaction.

[B]   Contiguous Property Owner Defense

The Brownfields Act provides a defense to liability for a party who owns property that is contiguous to, or similarly situated with respect to, contaminated property not owned by that party when hazardous substances migrate onto the real property from that off-site source. Generally, in order to be eligible for liability protection, a contiguous property owner must have satisfied many of the same conditions as the bona fide prospective purchaser. Additionally, in order to qualify for the liability protection, the contiguous property owner must not have caused, contributed, or consented to the release. The contiguous property owner must take reasonable steps with respect to the real property, to prevent and stop any release and prevent or limit human, environmental, or natural resource exposure to any hazardous substance that migrated onto the property.

At the time of acquisition, the contiguous property owner must have conducted all appropriate inquiry and must not have known, or have had reason to know, that the property was or could be contaminated by a release of hazardous substances from other real property not owned or operated by the contiguous property owner. In other words, a contiguous property owner would have to be an innocent landowner in order to qualify for this liability protection. However, the statute provides that any person that does not qualify for liability protection as a contiguous property owner may qualify for liability protection as a bona fide prospective purchaser.

The statute also provides that a contiguous property owner cannot be required to conduct a groundwater investigation or install a groundwater remediation system solely to address the migration of contamination in an aquifer, except in accordance with the EPA's May 24, 1995, policy concerning owners of property situated on contaminated aquifers. This policy document generally provides that the EPA will not take enforcement action against a property owner to address groundwater contamination when the contamination has come to be located on the property solely as a result of subsurface migration, unless the property owner is otherwise liable.

§ 11.04   STATE "SUPERFUND" AND LIEN LAWS

Page 746, add to note 21:

See, e.g., Fireman's Fund Ins. Co. v. City of Lodi, Cal., 41 F. Supp. 2d 1100 (E.D. Cal. 1999), *aff'd in part and rev'd in part*, 302 F.3d 928 (2002).

Page 747, add to note 25:

See also In re 229 Main St. Ltd. Partnership v. Massachusetts Dept. of Envtl. Protection, 262 F.3d 1 (1st Cir. 2001). In a case of first impression for the circuit courts, the First Circuit held that the automatic stay provision of the Bankruptcy Code does not prevent a state from perfecting its super-priority lien post-petition.

§ 11.06   CONTRACTUAL REALLOCATION OF LIABILITY

Page 750, add to note 31:

See generally Foster v. United States, 130 F. Supp. 2d 68 (D.D.C. 2001). The court determined that the transfer of property in "as is" condition did not result in an assumption of risk for contamination that the buyer did not know of at the time of the transfer.

Page 751, add to note 36:

Waste Management of Alameda County, Inc. v. East Bay Regional Park Dist., 135 F. Supp. 2d 1071 (N.D. Cal. 2001) (in order to shift CERCLA liability, a contract must directly, clearly, and unambiguously address the issue).

Page 751, add new note 39.1 at the end of the last paragraph:

... land and bind successors on title and interest.[39.1]

[39.1] *But see In the Matter of El Paso Refinery, LP*, 302 F.3d 343 (5th Cir. 2002); *Calabrese v. McHugh*, 170 F. Supp. 2d 243 (D. Conn. 2001). In *El Paso Refinery*, the Fifth Circuit examined a covenant in a deed that provided that the grantee would never attempt to compel the grantor to undertake any remedial or response action concerning environmental contamination on the property, and would not seek damages therefor. The case concerned a claim against the seller by a subsequent property owner for damages relating to environmental contamination, and whether the covenant in the deed precluded the subsequent property owner's claim. The Fifth Circuit examined whether the covenant was a real covenant running with the land, and therefore binding on the subsequent property owner, or, alternatively, whether the covenant was an equitable servitude and thereby binding upon the subsequent owner. The court concluded that the covenant did not touch and concern the land because it neither conveyed any benefit nor imposed any burden on the land. Rather, the covenant only benefited the grantor personally, and therefore did not touch and concern the land. As such, the covenant was not a real covenant running with the land. For the same reason, the court determined that the covenant was not an equitable servitude since an equitable servitude "must still 'concern the land or its use or enjoyment.' " In the *Calabrese case*, the court determined that an acknowledgement by a Grantee within a deed of the Grantor's dumping activities, and a covenant within that deed, not to sue for such activities, which covenant by its terms was binding on the Grantee's successors and assigns, was personal in nature, did not "touch and concern" the land, and was not "appurtenant" to the land. Consequently, the release was not binding upon a subsequent owner of the property that acquired the property without actual knowledge of the deed provision. The court noted that it was not deciding what impact actual knowledge of a subsequent purchaser of the deed provision would have in a future case involving the same facts.

Page 751, add at end of page:

In a decision that will challenge the drafting techniques of, and produce nightmares for, all real estate counsel, the U.S. District Court for the Northern District of Alabama held that a seller of real estate that agreed to remediate contamination "at its sole expense" waived its right to bring a CERCLA contribution action against its predecessor in title and other potentially responsible parties. *Southdown v. Allen*, 119 F. Supp. 2d 1223 (N.D. Ala. 2000). Plaintiffs brought a suit against the predecessor in title, Les Allen ("Allen"), who sold the plaintiffs all of the stock in Allworth, Inc. ("Allworth"). As a result of the stock sale, the plaintiffs acquired Allworth, which owned and operated a hazardous waste recycling facility.

All of the issued and outstanding shares of Allworth, in turn, were sold to Nortru, Inc. ("Nortru"), pursuant to a Stock Purchase Agreement ("Stock Agreement").[39.2]

In accordance with the terms of the Stock Agreement, the parties entered into a Remediation Agreement.[39.3] Pursuant to the Remediation Agreement, SETS agreed, "at its sole expense," to remediate all known contamination and all unknown contamination discovered during the cleanup of the known contamination. *Southdown*, 119 F. Supp. 2d at 1226. The Remediation Agreement also included a broad indemnity by SETS, in favor of Nortru, for any loss resulting from its performance or breach of its obligations under the Remediation Agreement. The Stock Agreement contained a broad indemnity in favor of Nortru, in part, for environmental claims relating to the contamination. SETS and SES also agreed within the Stock Agreement to a noncompete provision that stated, in part, that a portion of the value of the stock was attributable to the business relationship with Allworth's customers.

After Southdown filed suit, it amended its complaint to name certain current and former customers of Allworth. Allen responded to the complaint by filing a third-party complaint against Allworth and Nortru and a cross-claim against the current and former Allworth customers. The current and former Allworth customers, in turn, filed an action against additional current and former customers of Allworth. Nortru and Allworth filed a motion for partial summary judgment, and Southdown cross-moved for summary judgment. Allen and the third-party defendants joined in the Nortru and Allworth motion.

The central issue before the court was whether Southdown was barred from pursuing any cost recovery claim, since the Remediation Agreement provided for the cleanup to be performed at Southdown's "sole expense." Southdown argued that the contract provision was intended only to address the respective liability of the contracting parties. Nortru and Allworth, however, argued that the term "sole expense" meant that only Southdown would pay for the remediation.

Applying Texas law, the court determined that the words "sole expense" were clear on their face. Consequently, the court would not allow parole evidence to establish that the term "sole expense" should be limited in application to the contracting parties, rather than being extended to those who are not a party to the Remediation Agreement. The decision reflects the court's clear desire to preserve the integrity of the business acquisition. Because the suit resulted in claims against the Allworth customers, which could materially interfere with the business relationship with those customers, the court reasoned that the suit violated the covenant not to compete. Also, because of the broad indemnifications set forth in the agreements, the suit would only come full circle back to Southdown, since Nortru could advance a claim for indemnification inasmuch as the suit against Nortru related to the environmental conditions with respect to which Southdown provided an indemnity.

In reaching its decision, the court circumvented the express language of the agreements, which provided that the agreements were not intended to benefit anyone other than the contracting parties. As such, Southdown argued that neither Allen nor the Allworth customers should benefit from the cleanup obligation undertaken by Southdown in the agreements. The court determined that under Texas law a contract can incidentally benefit a person that is not a party to, and cannot enforce, a contract. Employing that logic, the court concluded that a contract can also benefit a third party even when the contracting parties did not intend to confer a benefit upon such third party. Consequently, the court allowed Allen and the current and former customers of Allworth to rely upon the contract language in order to avoid liability to Southdown.

Finally, the court determined that by using the "sole expense" language, Southdown expressly waived its right to contribution against Allen and the Allworth customers under CERCLA. According to the court, the only way for Southdown to have retained the right to sue others was for Southdown to have expressly retained its right to sue for contribution under CERCLA.

As a result of the *Southdown* decision, when a seller, buyer, landlord, or tenant undertakes to remediate a site, it should not use terms such as "at the expense of " or "at the sole cost or expense of " or similar language. Rather, the party agreeing to cleanup should express the obligation by providing that the remediation will be performed "at no cost or expense" to the other contracting party. In addition, and in order to be perfectly secure in light of the *Southdown* decision, it is recommended that the obligor expressly reserve the right to bring any claims it may have against others by way of contribution, indemnification, or otherwise, under common law or statute, regardless of whether the claim or cause of action now exists or is subsequently created or enacted. On the other hand, the beneficiary of such cleanup obligation should consider addressing expressly the issue of indemnification by the obligor in the event the beneficiary is brought into the action as a responsible party by virtue of its present owner or operator status.

[39.2] The plaintiffs in the action are Southdown, Inc., and Southdown Environmental LLC ("SELLC"). The Stock Agreement was entered into by Southdown Environmental

Treatment Systems, Inc. ("SETS"), and Southdown Environmental Systems, Inc. ("SES"). Southdown, Inc., guaranteed the obligations of SETS and SES. SETS merged into SELLC. The court referred to all of the plaintiffs as "Southdown," and the plaintiffs will be referred to herein in the same manner.

39.3 The Remediation Agreement was entered into only by SETS. Southdown, Inc., guaranteed the obligations of SETS.

§ 11.07   DUE DILIGENCE

Page 756, replace note 41 with:

Foster v. United States, 922 F. Supp. 642 (D.D.C., 1996). *But see Lefebvre v. Central Me. Power Co.*, 7 F. Supp. 2d 64 (D. Me. 1998); *United States v. Pacific Hide & Fur Depot*, 716 F. Supp. 1341 (D. Idaho 1989).

[B]   Federal, State, and Local Records Review

Page 763, add before penultimate sentence of text portion of subsection:

Also, the EPA's Web site should be reviewed, since the Web site has a database that can be used to search for environmental information about properties by inputting zip codes and local addresses. The EPA Web site is *www.epa.gov/echo.*

§ 11.09   DISCLOSURE AND TRANSACTION-TRIGGERED LAWS

Page 780, add after second paragraph:

It is important that real estate counsel recognize that a disclosure obligation may also arise from non-environmental statutes. For example, in New Jersey, the legislature adopted the New Residential Construction Off-Site Conditions Disclosure Act ("Disclosure Act"), N.J. Stat. Ann. § 46:3C-1 to -12, which limits the disclosure obligation of a seller of new residential construction. However, in *Nobrega v. Edison Glen Associates*, 327 N.J. Super. 415 (App. Div.), *cert. granted*, 165 N.J. 137 (2000), the appellate court held that although a developer may comply with the Disclosure Act, liability for failing to disclose off-site environmental conditions can attach under the state's Consumer Fraud Act, N.J. Stat. Ann. § 56:8-1 to -20. *Nobrega v. Edison Glenn Assocs.*, 327 N.J. Super. 415 (App. Div. 2000), was modified and remanded to the trial court by the

New Jersey Supreme Court. *Nobrega v. Edison Glenn Assocs.*, 167 N.J. 520 (2001). The court determined that the Disclosure Act prospectively precluded purchasers of newly constructed residential real estate from suing under the State's Consumer Fraud Act.

Page 781, add to note 66:

Hawaii Environmental Disclosure Law, Haw. Rev. Stat. Ann. §§ 343D-1 to -11, repealed June 14, 2001, by Act 247, 2001 Haw. Sess. Laws; Illinois Responsible Property Transfer Act of 1988 ch. 765, Ill. Comp. Stat. Ann. §§ 90/1-90/7, repealed Aug. 9, 2001, by P.A. 92-0299.

§ 11.11   LANDLORD AND TENANT ISSUES

[B]   Environmental Compliance Issues

Page 794, add new note 72.1 at end of third sentence of the second full paragraph:

... is being used and maintained in compliance with environmental laws.[72.1]

[72.1] *See New York v. Green*, 96 N. Y.2d 403, 754 N.E.2d 179, 729 N.Y.S.2d 420 (Ct. App. 2001) wherein the court determined that a landlord is liable for the activities of its tenants resulting in a discharge of contaminants on the landlord's property when the landlord has control over the activities of the tenant and has reason to believe the tenant will be using contaminants on the rental property.

Page 795, add new note 73.1 at end of first sentence of the first full paragraph:

... until all environmental activities are completed.[73.1]

[73.1] *But see River Road Assocs. v. Chesapeake Display and Packaging Co., Inc.*, 104 F. Supp. 2d 418 (D.N.J. 2000), wherein the court determined that a provision in a lease permitting the landlord to reinstate the lease upon its expiration if the tenant fails to return the leasehold in a condition required by the lease terms is an unenforceable penalty.

Page 795, add new note 73.2 at end of second sentence of the first full paragraph:

... with the environmental requirements of the lease.[73.2]

73.2 *See NRC Corp. v. Amoco Oil Co.*, 205 F.3d 1007 (7th Cir. 2000), wherein the court held that, on the basis of the broad lease indemnity, the tenant was liable to the landlord for loss of the use of property owned by the landlord and contiguous to the leasehold estate, even though the contamination did not migrate beyond the leasehold estate.

§ 11.12 ENVIRONMENTAL RISK INSURANCE

Page 806, add at end of section: *

An environmental insurance policy is written for a term of years, and a one-time premium is paid when the policy is issued. Although the per square foot cost of a policy, when amortized over the life of a policy, may be small, there is nevertheless a significant up-front capital expenditure. Other than contractor's pollution legal liability insurance, which is available on an "occurrence" basis, most types of coverage are written on a "claims made" basis. As such, coverage will be available only for a claim made and reported to the carrier during the policy period, or in some instances during an extended reporting period. It is therefore important to evaluate properly the length of the policy term when acquiring an environmental insurance policy.

[A]   Types of Coverage

The increased demand for environmental insurance has resulted in a tremendous growth in the various forms of environmental insurance coverage now available in the market. Although some carriers limit the number of types of policies they issue, others are continuing to expand on their offerings, showing an ever-increasing degree of creativity to meet the market's growing demand.

This section will focus on the main environmental insurance coverage offerings — namely, pollution legal liability insurance, cost overrun insurance, brownfield insurance, and secured creditor insurance.

---

* Sections [A] through [E] were adapted from an article by the author and Ann M. Waeger, Esq., initially presented in *The ACREL Papers — Fall 2000*, published by the American Law Institute American Bar Association, titled "The Emerging Role of Environmental Insurance in Commercial Real Estate Transactions: Issues and Answers."

Insurance carriers refer to these forms of coverage by different names, and some offer variations on the same theme, depending on the risk involved. There are also many additional types of environmental insurance policies available. They include:

- Storage tank pollution liability insurance

- Closure and post-closure care insurance

- Contractor's pollution liability insurance

- General contractor's pollution liability insurance

- Professional pollution liability insurance

- Commercial general liability insurance with contractor's pollution and professional liability insurance

- Commercial general liability insurance with pollution liability insurance

- Marina pollution liability insurance

- Agribusiness pollution liability insurance

- Dealer and repair pollution liability insurance

- Portfolio pollution liability insurance

- Asbestos pollution liability insurance

- Lead abatement contractors pollution liability insurance.

[B] Pollution Legal Liability Insurance

Pollution legal liability insurance is the generic designation for the type of insurance issued by all insurance carriers that is designed to provide coverage for on-site cleanup costs, claims for off-site cleanup costs, and claims for on-site and off-site bodily injury and property damage resulting from a pollution incident. This type of insurance also includes legal defense costs (which will be both subject to and deducted from policy limits) and may include business interruption and extra expense coverage, as well as diminution in property value due to a pollution incident. Coverage is available for preexisting and new conditions on a site, and depending on site conditions, coverage may be available for known conditions (for example, where contamination has been left in place with government permission and is being controlled by way of engineering controls, such as a cap).

Some insurance carriers have multiple policies for this generic type of coverage. Which policy the carrier will issue depends on the risk involved in the particular transaction and the coverage desired by the insured. For example, Gulf Insurance Company offers a policy entitled "Property Owner's Policy" and a policy entitled "Pollution Legal Liability Policy"; Zurich Insurance Company offers policies entitled "Real Estate Environmental Liability Insurance," "Environmental Cleanup and Liability Insurance," and "Environmental Impairment Liability Insurance"; AIG Environmental offers a policy entitled "Commercial Pollution Legal Liability" and a policy entitled "Commercial Real Estate Pollution Legal Liability"; and Kemper Environmental Ltd. offers policies entitled "Environmental Response, Compensation and Liability Insurance," "Environmental Liability Insurance," and "Environmental Insurance for Real Property Transfer." These policies differ in that some are designed for low-risk properties (such as office buildings) and provide broader coverage, by way of either a more expansive insuring agreement or fewer policy exclusions, while others are designed for medium- or high-risk properties (such as manufacturing facilities) and provide a narrower scope of coverage.

Each of the insurance carriers has its own set of minimums with respect to policy deductibles, but by way of a broad generalization, policy deductibles range from $5,000 to $10,000. Likewise, policies can be written for a term of up to 10 years and policy limits of up to $100 million per occurrence and $200 million in the aggregate. Most insurance carriers will require a Phase I site assessment before issuing a policy, although in certain situations additional site investigation may be required. Some insurance carriers will require only a database search and a transaction screen before issuing a policy. The deductible, amount of coverage, term of coverage, site conditions, and surrounding site conditions will all influence the policy premium.

Some insurance carriers will provide pollution legal liability protection for portfolios of real estate under a single policy. This provides the real estate investor the benefit of negotiating only one policy. There are a number of issues that must be addressed, however, when negotiating a portfolio-type policy, including the conditions under which newly acquired properties can be added to the policy and the cost for adding newly acquired properties to the policy.

[C] Cost Overrun Insurance

Cost overrun insurance, which is also known as stop gap, cleanup cap, cleanup cost containment, and remediation stop loss insurance, is designed to cover an increase in the cost of a known cleanup due to cost overruns. Typically, cost overrun insurance is issued when a policyholder has completed a site investigation and has received an approval from a governmental authority of its remedial action plan. Today, however, many insurance carriers have their own risk control groups and will issue coverage if their risk control group is satisfied with the cleanup plan.

A critical issue that must be examined when negotiating a cost overrun policy is what events and circumstances will be covered as "cost overruns." For example, will the policy cover the increase in the cost of a cleanup if the increase is due to the following events or conditions:

- Higher concentrations of contaminants already noted in the cleanup plan,

- The broader presence of known contaminants,

- Newly discovered contamination within or outside of already identified areas of concern,

- Broader cleanup requirements due to a change in regulatory requirements,

- Failure of a cleanup plan,

- Failure of a cleanup system,

- Negligence of the environmental consultant, or

- Unexpected geological conditions?

Depending on the insurance carrier, policy limits for cost overrun insurance can be as high as $100 million per occurrence and $200 million in the aggregate, and policies can be written for a term of 1 to 10 years, and possibly longer if an insurer can obtain reinsurance for the risk. These policies are written on a "claims made" basis. Consequently, when determining a policy term, an insured must consider whether the site will be the subject of a development and whether part of the development (such as improvements to be built) will serve as an engineering control in connection with the cleanup, thereby requiring the insured to account for the time period for obtaining development approvals and constructing the improvements. Notwithstanding the policy term, cost overrun coverage normally will end when a No Further Action Letter is issued for the cleanup (if that takes place prior to the expiration of the policy term). It is important that the policy be negotiated so that post–No Further Action Letter requirements (such as continued monitoring) are covered. In addition, the cost overrun policy will contain a self-insured retention, which normally will equal the estimated cost of a cleanup plus a multiple (10 or 20 percent) of the estimated cost of cleanup. Policy premiums generally will be a percentage of the estimated cost of cleanup, although the setting of the premium will be affected by the limits of liability, the self-insured retention, the nature and anticipated duration of the cleanup, and the remediation contractor.

There is an increasing trend today for environmental cleanup contractors to quote fixed-price cleanups. This phenomenon is a result of the increased competition between environmental remediation contractors and the fact that the industry has gained greater experience in the nature of cleanups and the unknowns typically encountered during cleanups. To protect themselves, however, and at the same time provide a comfort level to the property owner, such contractors in many instances purchase cost overrun insurance.

[D] Brownfield Insurance

Brownfield insurance is a policy that combines both pollution legal liability insurance and cost overrun insurance into one policy. A brownfield type of policy is the preferred choice where an insured is redeveloping a site on which a cleanup must be performed. The insured can better protect against a gap in coverage that easily can result if two different policies must be negotiated, with potentially two different sets of definitions, exclusions, and conditions.

[E] Secured Creditor Insurance

Secured creditor insurance is a relatively new environmental insurance product. Although much of the lending community's concern for environmental liability was addressed by the federal and state governments with the enactment of a variety of lender liability protections, the lending community still has had concerns over environmental issues and their potential impact on a credit facility. These concerns relate to questions regarding the borrower's ability to meet its debt service obligations if faced with a costly cleanup during the life of a loan and the lender's ability to realize the full value from its collateral if the collateral is tainted by environmental contamination.

Depending on the insurance carrier issuing the policy, coverage under the secured creditor policy can be as high as $100 million per occurrence and $200 million in the aggregate, and the policy term can be as long as 20 years. Again depending on the insurance carrier, the policy can be written to cover first-party cleanup costs, claims for third-party cleanup costs, claims for third-party bodily injury and property damage, legal defense costs, and payment of the outstanding loan balance. Typically, a secured creditor policy has been written to cover the lesser of the loan balance (provided there was a default under the loan) or cleanup costs (provided there was a foreclosure). Now, however, coverage is available to recover the loan balance after default if there has been a pollution condition at the collateralized property.

Generally, the insurance carriers will issue secured creditor policies based on a transaction screen and a database search, although a Phase I site investigation may be required depending on the size of the loan and the operations conducted on the secured property. Insurance carriers are also providing such coverage on a portfolio basis, so that a lender can add properties to the policy as new loans are closed. In addition, insurance carriers are marketing the insurance as an alternative to a Phase I site assessment. The coverage can be bound faster than the time period normally required to perform a Phase I site investigation, and the cost of the coverage is less than the cost for a Phase I site investigation. As a result, the borrower can save money and close the loan sooner than where a lender requires a Phase I site assessment.

Secured creditor policies have become particularly important in securitized loan transactions. Certain rating agencies, such as Fitch IBCA and Moody's Investors Service, will give additional credit support to commercial mortgaged-backed securities pools that use environmental insurance.

[F] Institutional Control Environmental Insurance

Institutional Control Environmental Insurance is a special niche policy recently created by Zurich Insurance Company to cover four types of risks associated with institutional and engineering controls. The first insures against cost overruns in the design and implementation of institutional controls. Second is coverage for errors and omissions by the professionals who design and establish the controls, which includes coverage for bodily injury, property damage, and cleanup costs. Third is coverage against failure of a properly designed system of engineering and institutional controls, for example, where there is a change in site conditions. Finally, the policy will cover against bodily injury, property damage, and cleanup costs arising out of an error or omission by the professionals who are responsible for maintaining or enforcing engineering and institutional controls.

[G] Policy Exclusions*

The insuring agreement section of a policy sets forth the coverage that will be afforded by a policy. The exclusion section of a policy, however, is the heart of the policy, for it is here that the insurance carrier narrows and removes coverage ostensibly afforded by the insuring agreement. Consequently, the exclusions must be examined with utmost care.

[1] Known Conditions Exclusion

In a decision involving a contemporary environmental insurance policy, the United States District Court for the Eastern District of Pennsylvania, in *Goldenberg Development Corp., et al. v. Reliance Insurance Co., for Illinois*, No. 00-CV-3055, 2001 U.S. Dist. LEXIS 12870 (E.D. Pa. 2001), interpreted a policy exclusion, namely, the known conditions exclusion. The court determined that the disclosure of environmental reports does not constitute disclosure of "facts" for purposes of the known conditions exclusion. Prior to this decision, the critical issue that frequently arose in the context of the known conditions exclusion concerned what constituted a known condition and whose knowledge was relevant in determining what conditions would be deemed known conditions. However, maybe even more important now, is the manner in which the insured discloses those conditions that are in fact known to the insured prior to the policy inception.

This decision brings to a head a difficult issue facing prospective insureds. Insurers expect and require an insured to disclose all material facts known to the insured prior to the inception of a policy. However, it is now arguable that the insured undertake the obligation of reviewing and summarizing all environmental conditions disclosed in all known environmental reports.

Frequently, real estate counsel's involvement in the environmental insurance policy process follows the application stage. However, because disclosure of a known condition must be made during the application process, this decision now makes it incumbent upon real estate counsel to review the application and environmental reports filed with the carrier, and examine closely with the client and its environmental consultant, the environmental conditions known to exist at the subject property, to ensure

---

* This section was adapted from an article by the author initially presented in *ACREL News*, Vol. 19, No. 4 (Dec. 2001).

that full and proper disclosure of all material facts was made by the insured during the application process. Alternatively, if the quantity of environmental reports makes this task impracticable, then real estate counsel must negotiate a provision in the policy, that will deem disclosed all conditions identified in documents delivered to the insurer prior to the policy inception, and must require that a list of such documents be appended to the policy.

[2] Mold Exclusion

Claims for bodily injury, property damage, and cleanup costs arising out of mold have become the new hot topic for insurance companies over the last year. Mold is present in the environment and individuals live with mold on a daily basis, generally with no adverse affect. However, because claims against general liability and first-party property damage policies are on such a rise, and have resulted in staggering verdicts in favor of insureds, certain insurers issuing environmental insurance policies have begun automatically including exclusions for mold in their premium indication for each new policy. Insureds may find that depending upon the risk, underwriters will agree to add this coverage back to the policy by offering a sub-limit of coverage for an additional premium.

[H] Government Led Insurance Programs

Massachusetts, California, Connecticut, and Wisconsin have started incentive programs to foster the use of environmental insurance to stimulate the cleanup and redevelopment of Brownfield sites. These state programs feature pre-negotiated policies, subsidies, and access to consultants.

California and Massachusetts offer programs that focus on pollution cleanup liability cost caps for borrowers where there is a high risk of contamination. For example, Massachusetts Brownfield Redevelopment Access to Capital Program (BRAC) subsidizes eligible borrower's insurance premiums by 25 percent in addition to offering pre-negotiated policies specifically designed for BRAC. California's Financial Assurance and Insurance for Redevelopment Program (FAIR Program) includes pollution legal liability, cost overrun, and secured creditor insurance. The FAIR Program also provides subsidies that may be used to offset the costs of premiums and deductibles. Through a competitive bidding process, on June 9, 2003, California provisionally selected AIG Environmental as the insurance carrier for its FAIR program.

By contrast, Connecticut's Special Contaminated Property Remediation and Insurance Fund provides loans and technical assistance to eligible participants seeking to purchase policies instead of a pre-negotiated policy package that is actually available for purchase.

Wisconsin's insurance program is a component of the state Department of Natural Resources (DNR) Voluntary Cleanup Program (VCP) for contaminated groundwater. A participant relying on natural attenuation for groundwater restoration prior to achieving compliance with groundwater enforcement standards may pay a one-time insurance fee to the state to enter into the program. The DNR calculates individual fees according to its published fee schedule, which is based on the previous uses of the property (*i.e.*, agricultural, industrial, or residential) and acreage. This fee qualifies the participant upon completion of the program to qualify for a transferable certificate of completion, providing relief from future liability to the voluntary party and any successors or assignees. If natural attenuation fails, the DNR may file a claim where the state pays a deductible and the insurer pays the remaining amount for site assessments, onsite, and offsite cleanup. The voluntary party who performed the original cleanup is not required to file a claim or pay any additional costs.

CHAPTER 12
INDUSTRIAL LEASES
Philip D. Weller

Page 816, at the end of text of § 12.03, before Form 12-3:

Many sophisticated tenants are requesting that the landlord put a ceiling on the amount of operating expenses that may be passed through the sort of provision described above. Landlords, depending on the tenant and the market, may be amenable to this, but generally will not agree to putting a limit on increases that are not within their control, such as taxes, insurance, and utility costs. **Form 12-4A**, this supplement, provides an example of a provision limiting the increases in controllable operating costs that may be passed through under a lease.

Page 817, add alternative to current Form 12-3, Basic Rent Provisions:

[Alternative 2]

§ _____ Basic Rent Provisions—Statement of Estimated Expense Charges Included

Initial Monthly Base Rent:			$_____
Initial Estimated Monthly Operating Expense Payments: (estimates only and subject to adjustment to actual costs and expenses according to the provisions of this Lease)	1. Utilities	$_____	
	2. Common Area Charges	$_____	
	3. Taxes	$_____	
	4. Insurance	$_____	
	5. Others: Mgmt. Fees	$_____	
	_____	$_____	
	_____	$_____	
Initial Estimated Monthly Operating Expense Payments			$_____
Initial Monthly Base Rent and Operating Expense Payments			$_____

[Note: This provision would be combined with Form 12-4 regarding operating expense pass-through provisions.]

Page 819, add new Form 12-4A at end of Form 12-4:

FORM 12-4A
LIMIT ON INCREASES IN CONTROLLABLE OPERATING EXPENSES

§ _____ *Controllable Operating Expenses*

For the purposes of this provision, the term "*Controllable Operating Expenses*" shall mean all Operating Expenses other than (1) Taxes; (2) the costs of all utilities used in the Building that are not billed separately to a tenant of the Building for above–Building — standard utility consumption; and (3) the cost of insurance. **[Alternative Provision — Some landlords may wish to include management fees as Operating Expenses that are not subject to the limitation on increases.]**

Notwithstanding the provisions of Section _____ regarding the payment of Operating Expenses, Controllable Operating Expenses in any calendar year shall not increase by more than ____% per annum during each calendar year in the Term (which amount shall be compounded annually on a cumulative basis from the first calendar year during the Term).

Page 849, add new section:

§ 12.15　CONDEMNATION AND CASUALTY PROVISIONS THAT SHIFT RISK TO THE TENANT

In drafting industrial leases that the lending community will treat (and price) as being completely "bondable," it may be necessary to include a provision that effectively shifts most of the risk of a casualty or condemnation loss to the tenant. The lender's reasoning is that it is relying primarily on the credit of the tenant in providing the financing — in fact, such financing may be more properly considered an unsecured credit loan to the tenant than a secured mortgage loan to the landlord/developer. Accordingly, the lender wishes the lease to be "bondable" in the sense that the rent stream under the lease will be paid as reliably as interest and principal would be payable on a bond issued by the tenant. While the typical limitations on landlord's remedies in many states, of course, have an impact on the lender's evaluation of the credit risk (*see* § 12.11 in the main volume), the typical casualty and condemnation loss provisions will give the lender greater problems in this type of financing transaction. *See* **Forms 12-12** and **12-22** in the main volume for typical casualty and taking/condemnation provisions. The reason that casualty and condemnation provisions are of greater concern in this regard is that they arise from events beyond the control of the landlord or tenant — the risk that the tenant will not pay the rent is essentially the same credit risk as nonpayment of principal or interest. The more typical lease allocation of risk in the case of a casualty or condemnation places much of the economic burden on the landlord, rather than on the tenant, where the lender wishes it to be placed.

Form 12-24, this supplement, reflects an alternate condemnation and casualty provision that effectively shifts the risk of a casualty or condemnation loss to the tenant. Basically, the form obligates the tenant to either restore or irrevocably offer to acquire the landlord's interest in the premises remaining after the taking or casualty for a purchase price that, when coupled with the attendant casualty insurance proceeds or condemnation award, is at least sufficient to pay the outstanding balance of the financing secured by the property. This is often accomplished by attaching a schedule to the lease, very similar in form to an amortization schedule, which lists specified termination dates and provides for the payment on those dates of an amount, a "termination value," sufficient to pay at least the outstanding balance of financing in full. If the landlord has contributed a significant amount of equity to the project, the schedule for the termination values should also, from the landlord's perspective, be negotiated so as to provide for the return of as much of the unamortized equity as possible. In a build-to-suit situation, the goals of the lender and the landlord can also be readily achieved by tying the termination values to the cost of the facility, with appropriate amortization over the term of the lease. A note of caution: The tenant's desire to treat the lease as a true lease for tax and accounting purposes can be impacted depending on the length of the term and the extent that risk of loss is placed on the tenant, and advice of tax counsel should be sought in connection with such provisions to be sure that the desired treatment of the lease, from both the landlord's and the tenant's perspectives, is achieved.

FORM 12-24
CONDEMNATION AND CASUALTY DAMAGE PROVISION — ENTIRE RISK SHIFTED TO TENANT

§ _____ *Condemnation and Casualty.*

(a) Tenant hereby assigns to Landlord any award, compensation, insurance proceeds, or other payment to which Tenant may become entitled by reason of its interest in the Premises other than any award, compensation, or insurance payment made to Tenant for interruption or loss of business, for moving expenses, or for any inventory, machinery, equipment, or other personal property belonging to Tenant, including, without limitation, Tenant's equipment (hereinafter referred to as *"Tenant's Loss"*) by reason of (1) damage to or destruction of the Premises by fire or other casualty or cause (a *"Casualty"*), or (2) any condemnation, requisition, or other taking or sale of the use, occupancy, or title to the Premises or any portion thereof in, by, or on account of any actual or threatened eminent domain proceeding or other action by any governmental authority or other person having the power of eminent domain (a *"Condemnation"*). Tenant is hereby authorized and empowered, at its sole cost and expense, in the name and on behalf of Landlord, Tenant, or otherwise, to appear in any such proceeding or other action; to negotiate, accept, and prosecute any claim for any award, compensation, insurance proceeds, or other payment on account of any such casualty or condemnation; and to cause any such award, compensation, insurance proceeds, or other payments to be paid to Landlord, except that Tenant shall be entitled to submit a separate claim for Tenant's Loss and receive and retain any award applicable thereto. All amounts so paid or payable to Landlord or Tenant shall be retained or paid over to the party entitled thereto in accordance with the provisions of this Section. Tenant shall take all appropriate action in connection with each such claim, proceeding, or other action. Landlord and Landlord's Mortgagee *[Note: see Form 12-18, in the main volume, for a definition of "Landlord's Mortgagee"]* may participate in such proceedings, and Tenant shall deliver all instruments reasonably requested by Landlord or Landlord's Mortgagee to permit such participation, and shall pay all costs and expenses reasonably incurred in connection therewith.

(b)   If less than substantially all of the Premises shall be damaged or destroyed by Casualty, or Condemned, then Tenant shall give prompt written notice thereof to Landlord, and this Lease shall continue in full force and effect, and Tenant shall proceed at Tenant's own cost and expense and in conformity with the requirements set forth in Section _____ [reference section dealing with repairs and alterations] with reasonable diligence and promptness to carry out any necessary demolition and to restore, repair, replace, and/or rebuild the Premises in order to restore the Premises, as nearly as practicable, to substantially the same condition, design, and construction as that which existed immediately prior to such Casualty and Condemnation.

(c)   Base Rent shall not abate hereunder by reason of any such Casualty or Condemnation, and Tenant shall continue to perform and fulfill all of Tenant's obligations, covenants, and agreements hereunder notwithstanding the same.

(d)   Landlord and Tenant shall agree on the maximum cost of such restoration, repair, replacement, or rebuilding, such agreement not to be unreasonably withheld or delayed, and such cost shall be paid first out of Tenant's own funds to the extent such cost exceeds (1) in the case of a Casualty, the net insurance proceeds payable in respect thereof, or (2) in the case of a Condemnation, the net award payable in respect thereof (in either case, the *"Net Award"*), and then out of the Net Award. If Landlord and Tenant cannot agree on the maximum cost of such restoration, repair, replacement, or rebuilding, the issue shall be submitted to arbitration in accordance with the Commercial Arbitration Rules of the American Arbitration Association, on an expedited basis (*"Arbitration"*). The Net Award shall be made available to Tenant for restoration, repair, and rebuilding as follows: (i) if the Net Award does not exceed $_____ (the *"Alteration Cost Threshold"*), and provided that no Event of Default has occurred and is continuing, then the Net Award shall be paid to Tenant (and to the extent the Net Award was previously assigned to Landlord, it will be remitted by Landlord to Tenant) to be applied to the repair and rebuilding work required by this Section, or (ii) if the Net Award exceeds the Alteration Cost Threshold, the proceeds shall be disbursed in accordance with Subsection (g) below.

(e)   If at any time during the Term, Tenant shall reasonably determine that all or substantially all of the Premises have been destroyed by Casualty, or all or substantially all of the Premises have been taken by Condemnation, or after any substantial Condemnation of the Premises if the Premises are unsuitable for continued use in Tenant's business, Tenant shall notify Landlord of such event in writing within thirty (30) days of such Condemnation or Casualty. In such event Tenant may either (1) rebuild and/or restore the Premises at Tenant's own cost and expense and in accordance with the requirements set forth herein, or (2) give written notice to Landlord within ninety (90) days after such Condemnation or Casualty of Tenant's intention to terminate this Lease in conformity with the requirements set forth herein. Substantially all of the Premises shall be deemed to have been taken by Condemnation if the remaining portion shall not be of sufficient size or character to permit the operation by Tenant on an economically feasible basis of the business conducted thereon immediately prior to the Condemnation, assuming that such remaining portion had been repaired and restored to the fullest extent possible. Substantially all of the Premises shall be deemed to have been destroyed by Casualty, if, as to any one occurrence, _____ percent (_____%) or more of the total net rentable square foot area within the Premises shall be damaged or destroyed and Tenant determines in its reasonable discretion that the Premises are no longer suitable for use in its business. Tenant's notice to Landlord of Tenant's intent to terminate this Lease shall: (A) contain a brief description of the relevant Condemnation or Casualty; (B) specify a date for the termination of this Lease, which shall be the last day of a calendar month not less than 90 nor more than 120 days after such notice is given (the **"Termination Date"**); (C) if such notice of termination shall be based on a reasonable determination by Tenant that after such Casualty or Condemnation the Premises are no longer suitable for use in Tenant's business as aforesaid, contain a certification by Tenant that Tenant will discontinue the use of the Premises in Tenant's ordinary course of business; (D) contain the irrevocable offer of Tenant to purchase Landlord's interest in the Premises (and in the Net Award) on such Termination Date at the Termination Value (defined as the amount specified opposite the applicable Termination Date on Schedule _____ hereto *[Note: see comments in § 12.15, this supplement, for a description of this schedule]*); and (E) contain a commitment by Tenant to deposit with a Depository (defined below) not later than 90 days after the date of the Condemnation or Casualty (but not later than the Termination Date) as security for payment of the purchase price for the Premises the applicable Termination Value less the amount of any Net Award previously paid with respect to such Casualty or Condemnation and held by Landlord or Landlord's designee pursuant to this Section. If Landlord shall reject such offer to purchase by notice (countersigned by Landlord's Mortgagee) given to Tenant not later than thirty (30) days prior to such Termination Date, then this Lease shall terminate on such Termination Date and the Net Award shall be paid and belong to Landlord, plus an amount equal to the deductible payable under the policy or policies of insurance, which shall be paid by Tenant to Landlord. Unless Landlord shall reject such offer to purchase as provided in the preceding sentence, Landlord shall be conclusively deemed to have accepted such offer, and on such Termination Date Landlord shall transfer, and Tenant shall purchase, Landlord's interest in the Premises (and in the Net Award) and upon payment of the purchase price, Tenant's obligation to pay Base Rent shall terminate on the Termination Date. The additional amount, if any, deposited by Tenant pursuant to clause (E) preceding and not applied towards the purchase price of the Premises shall be paid to Tenant on the Termination Date provided that there is no Event of Default then existing. On the Termination Date Landlord shall execute a special warranty deed conveying to Tenant Landlord's interest in the Premises free and clear of all claims and encumbrances except those (excluding any liens) that encumber the Premises on the date hereof or are hereafter placed thereon by Landlord and that do not materially affect the use of the Premises contemplated by this Lease, and Tenant shall pay to Landlord the purchase price therefor.

(f)   If, following a Casualty or Condemnation, Tenant shall not give notice of its intention to terminate this Lease in accordance with Subsection (e) above or shall not be entitled to give notice of its intention to terminate this Lease, then this Lease shall continue in full force and effect.

(g)   If the Net Award shall exceed the Alteration Cost Threshold, or if an Event of Default has occurred and is continuing, then:

(1)   The full amount of the Net Award shall be paid to a depository (the **"*Depository*"**) to be selected as hereinafter provided. The Depository shall be Landlord's Mortgagee, or if there is no Landlord's Mortgagee, then the Depository shall be a bank or trust company selected by Landlord and approved by Tenant (so long as an Event of Default does not exist under this Lease) which approval shall not be unreasonably withheld or delayed. The Depository shall have no affirmative obligation to prosecute a determination of the amount of, or to effect the collection of, any insurance proceeds or condemnation award or awards, unless the Depository shall have been given an express written undertaking to do so by Landlord and Tenant. Moneys received by the Depository pursuant to the provisions of this Lease shall not be commingled with other funds and shall be held by the Depository in trust, either separately or with other trust funds, for the uses and purposes provided in this Lease. The Depository shall place any moneys held by it into an interest bearing account, and the interest paid or received by the Depository on the moneys so held in trust shall be added to the moneys so held in trust. The Depository shall not be liable or accountable for any action taken or suffered by the Depository or for any disbursement of moneys made by the Depository in good faith in reliance on advice of legal counsel. In disbursing moneys pursuant to Subsections (g)(2), (g)(3), and (g)(4) below, the Depository may rely conclusively on the information contained in any notice given to the Depository by Tenant in accordance with the provisions of such provision, unless Landlord shall notify the Depository in writing within five (5) business days after the giving of any such notice that Landlord intends to dispute such information, in which case the disputed amount shall not be disbursed but shall continue to be held by the Depository until such dispute shall have been resolved by agreement of the parties or by Arbitration;

(2)   Provided that no Event of Default has occurred and is continuing, from time to time, but not more than once in any thirty (30) day period, Tenant may request reimbursement out of the Net Award for the actual costs and expenses incurred by Tenant in connection with such repair and rebuilding. Such requests shall be made by written notice to the Depository, with a copy to Landlord, setting forth in reasonable detail all of such costs and expenses incurred by Tenant. If Landlord shall in good faith desire to dispute the information contained in any such notice given by Tenant, Landlord shall so notify Tenant and the Depository in writing within five (5) business days after the giving of such notice, specifying the amount intended to be disputed and the nature of the dispute. After such five (5) business day period has elapsed, if Landlord has not disputed the information contained in Tenant's Notice, the Depository shall promptly disburse to

Tenant out of the Net Award the amount of such costs and expenses. If Landlord disputes the information contained in Tenant's Notice, such dispute shall be resolved by agreement of the parties or by Arbitration, and any undisputed amount shall be released to Tenant;

(3) Upon the completion of such repair and rebuilding, any remaining Net Award shall be paid to and belong to Tenant; and

(4) Notwithstanding any other provision to the contrary contained in this Section, in the event of a temporary Condemnation, this Lease shall remain in full force and effect and Tenant shall be entitled to the Net Award allocable to such temporary Condemnation; except that such portion of the Net Award allocable to the time period after the expiration or termination of the Term of this Lease shall be paid to Landlord.

CHAPTER 14
OFFICE LEASES

§ 14.02   THE OFFICE TENANT'S QUESTIONS

Page 899, add new paragraph at end of section:

A very strong tenant may have a wish list in its request for proposal that is instructive for — but definitely not always applicable to — a smaller tenant. Depending upon the marketplace, the strong tenant may not be able to get all these agreements. In some markets, a smaller tenant may be able to get some of them. A very desirable tenant would like:

1. With regard to the premises:

   (a)   continuing rights of first refusal at the rental rate at the time the space is added in adjacent space including space on the same floor and floors above or below the premises, and perhaps on all space in the building;

   (b)   expansion options on adjacent space including space on the same floor and floors above or below the premises, and perhaps on all space in the building;

   (c)   storage space.

2. With regard to the term:

   (a)   a term and rent commencement date based upon substantial completion of the premises, exterior areas, and areas and service facilities (such as air conditioning and elevators), as evidenced by a certificate of occupancy and architect's certificate of completion, advance notice of substantial completion, and an opportunity to inspect the premises and verify the operability of the systems;

   (b)   a delay of term and rent commencement for *force majeure*, or any act attributable to the landlord or its contractors including slow response to changes and repair of non-conforming work;

    (c)   cancellation rights based upon the payment of, for example, six months' rent;

    (d)   numerous renewal options at fixed or indexed rental rates (but not market which may be too high);

    (e)   parking, both reserved and unreserved, at fixed or bargain rates, at a higher ratio of spaces to premises area than the landlord usually offers, at convenient locations designated by the tenant.

3.   With respect to operating expenses:

    (a)   a gross up of operating expenses to 100 percent;

    (b)   "caps" on operating expenses increases;

    (c)   audit rights with a right to charge the landlord for the cost of the audit if an error is found;

    (d)   numerous exclusions from operating expenses such as those set forth in **§ 14.10[B][2]**, main volume;

    (e)   no charge (or a fixed or bargain rate) for after-hours HVAC usage.

4.   With regard to tenant improvements:

    (a)   an allowance that covers all construction, permitting, and design costs;

    (b)   base building (that is, the landlord's work) that includes access to supplemental power if the tenant's floor is inadequate, telephone and other communication wiring, access to the landlord's emergency generators and fuel (or space at no cost for the tenant's own emergency generator and fuel supply), life support and security systems, adequate cooling, and other legal requirements such as ADA compliance;

    (c)   the tenant's free choice of architect, contractor, and subcontractors;

    (d)   the tenant's right to apply the allowance as it wishes (including as a credit against rent);

    (e)   the tenant's right to require the landlord's contractor to do the work, and no fee to the landlord for supervision in any case, in which event the tenant participates in the bidding (to at least three contractors and major subcontractors) and selection;

    (f)   free parking for the tenant's architect, contractor, and subcontractors during construction;

    (g)   free use of hoists, elevators, utilities and HVAC, loading docks;

    (h)   reserved elevators for the weekend when the tenant moves its personal property.

5.   With regard to the building:

    (a)   HVAC, electrical power, and janitorial service (with a right to do its own for a reduction of operating expenses attributable to janitorial), according to the tenant's specifications;

    (b)   services during the tenant's business hours and a limitation of the building "holidays";

    (c)   security services;

    (d)   access to the premises (and parking lot) at all times, the right to use stairwells between adjoining floors of the premises, and dedicated elevators;

    (e)   telecommunications antenna;

    (f)   free or bargain rate use of the building amenities (such as health club);

    (g)   building identity (that is, signage) or at least a restriction of others' signage (such as competitors), lobby, directory, elevator, and floor signage;

    (h)   professional building management consistent with the quality of the building;

    (i)   the landlord's representation regarding the absence of hazardous material and its promise to remediate at no cost to the tenant any that appears;

    (j)   the landlord's representation regarding the compliance with all laws (including ADA, OSHA, and building codes) and its promise to comply with them at no cost to the tenant.

6.   Unrestricted right of assignment or sublease without recapture or profit sharing.

7.   Unrestricted, or minimally restricted, right to make alterations to the premises.

8.   A waiver of the security deposit and any landlord's lien.

9. Rent abatement for interruption of services.

10. The tenant's right to any part of a condemnation award allocable to its furniture, fixtures, loss of good will, and moving expenses.

11. The tenant's right to self-insure.

12. Rights of offset for the landlord's defaults including its failure to pay the allowance.

13. Arbitration of disputes.

14. The landlord's responsibility for the tenant's broker's compensation.

15. A non-disturbance agreement from the landlord's lender.

16. A general requirement of reasonableness, promptness, and good faith when consents are required.

17. The use of the tenant's lease form.

CHAPTER 15
ASSIGNMENT OF LEASES

Stephen A. Linde
Martin P. Miner

Page 984, add new section before § 15.08:

§ 15.07A   "SNAP-BACK" ASSIGNMENTS

[A]   Introduction

A tenant that assigns a lease parts with its entire leasehold interest; the assignee replaces the assignor as tenant and the assignor retains no reversionary interest. However, absent a release by the landlord, the assignee remains fully liable to the landlord for the tenant's remaining obligations under the lease. Such liability survives the termination of the lease based on the tenant's default.

The proper allocation of responsibility to a landlord as between the assignor and assignee following an assignment is discussed in detail in § 15.04 in the main volume. As indicated in that section, the assignee's assumption of lease obligations provides the assignor a right of recovery against the assignee if the assignor is called upon by the landlord to satisfy lease obligations not paid or performed by the assignee. This right may provide insufficient comfort to an assigning tenant concerned about the creditworthiness of its assignee or the ability to locate the assignee following a default for which the landlord obtains a recovery from the assignor. In addition, the assignee's bankruptcy or insolvency may leave the assignor with a liability to the landlord and no source of recovery from the assignee.

The obvious solution for a tenant disposing of its leased space and having this concern is a sublease. The departing tenant retains a reversionary interest and may declare a default against, and evict, the defaulting subtenant and regain control of the space. Such control includes the sublandlord's ability to cover its liability to the landlord by re-leasing to a new subtenant, which may have a better credit or can provide a security deposit.

A sublease, however, may not be desirable or feasible in some cases. A tenant disposing of its space, and perhaps going out of business or leaving the area entirely, may be unable or unwilling to assume the burden of continuing administration of the main lease and a sublease, including receipt of rent bills, analysis of rent escalations and other non-fixed charges, and billing and collection under the sublease. Such a tenant is unlikely to devote the time of its personnel or incur the expense of an agent to perform these functions. Moreover, in the case of a corporate reorganization or sale of a business or division (whether through the sale of assets or ownership interests), keeping the assignor as an operating entity for the purpose of lease and sublease administration may be a case of "the tail wagging the dog." Unless the corporate transaction is real estate-driven, management probably will not be focusing on the leases and will desire only to be rid of them.

Similarly, a sublease may be unacceptable to the new party taking over the space. Such party may want to deal with the landlord directly rather than with a sublandlord that may be inactive or absent. It may view a direct landlord-tenant relationship with the building owner as more suited to making a long term deal to remain in the space when the lease expires. It may not want to bear the risk of the sublandlord's default under the main lease or its bankruptcy, as questions about its status in the space may interfere with the conduct of its business. Even though these concerns may be mitigated if the subtenant can obtain a non-disturbance or recognition agreement from the main landlord, or another agreement allowing it to remain in the space following the sublandlord's default or bankruptcy, such agreements, unlike a simple consent to a lease assignment, take time to draft and negotiate. Also, there may be no time for the negotiation of non-disturbance rights with landlords in the middle of a complicated corporate transaction that has to close under time pressure.

In short, if the new occupant of the space, for whatever reason, requires an assignment rather than a sublease in order to become a direct tenant of the building, it probably will not agree to a sublease solely to accommodate its transferor's concern about ongoing liability to the landlord.

[B] The Assignor Who Won't Let Go

For the departing tenant who does not want, or cannot obtain, a sublease to the new tenant, but desires the benefit of the reversionary interest inherent in a sublease, is there a way for it to "eat its cake and have it too"? One method that has been tried is the "snap-back" assignment. This device consists of a lease assignment and assumption together with a right on the part of the assignor to require the assignee to assign the lease back to the assignor in the event the assignee defaults. Upon such re-assignment, the assignor can again control the space, cure defaults, and assign to another party or sublease in order to avoid or minimize ongoing liability to the landlord. Such a re-assignment would, of course, only work if accomplished before the lease is terminated on the basis of the assignee/tenant's lease default. In the case of monetary defaults, such a termination presumably can be prevented by the assignor's delivery of a check to the landlord, whether or not the assignee complies with the obligation to re-assign.

A sample "snap-back" clause in an instrument of assignment and assumption might read as follows:

> In the event that Assignee defaults in the performance of any obligations under the Lease hereby assumed by Assignee, and such defaults are not cured within the notice and cure periods set forth in the Lease, Assignor may, upon two (2) days' prior notice to Assignee, terminate this Assignment and in such event Assignee shall immediately reassign the Lease to Assignor. In the event Assignee fails to reassign the Lease to Assignor as required by this Section, Assignee hereby appoints Assignor as Assignee's attorney-in-fact, which apportionment is coupled with an interest, to execute such re-assignment document on behalf of Assignee. In addition, in such event, Assignee shall immediately quit and peacefully surrender the Premises to Assignor, and Assignor and its agents may immediately, or at any time thereafter, without further notice, re-enter the Premises, either by summary proceedings or by any other applicable action or proceeding or otherwise, and remove all persons and property from the Premises. The terms "re-enter," "re-entry," or "reentered" as used in this Assignment shall not be deemed to be restricted to their technical legal meanings. No such reassignment shall relieve Assignee from any liability which Assignee may have to Assignor under this Assignment arising from Assignee's defaults under the Lease.

Under the above language, the assignor is out of the picture until something goes wrong. Then, the assignor has rights to terminate, an appointment as attorney-in-fact, and eviction rights. This arrangement resembles neither an assignment nor a sublease; it seems to have attributes of a deferred sublease taking effect at a future time. As such, both parties to such an arrangement, whether they realize it or not, are in a situation in which their legal status is uncertain.

Clearly, the assignor desires that the landlord include in its consent to the lease assignment an agreement to notify the assignor of any tenant default in order to permit the assignor to exercise the right to obtain the re-assignment in a timely manner. The landlord may or may not agree to this.

[C]   Legal Status of the "Snap-Back" Assignment

The legal issues raised by "snap-back" assignments are whether the assignor's right to compel a re-assignment is enforceable and whether this feature effectively recharacterizes the assignment as a sublease.

There is little authority offering guidance on these issues. *Friedman on Leases* provides that: "The usual form of assignment of lease passes the tenant's entire interest and makes no provision for defeasance. Even if [it] did the assignment would probably not qualify under the statutes that give possessory remedies to landlords." Milton R. Friedman, Friedman on Leases § 7.501d (4th ed. 1997). One New York case discusses an assignment as security for a loan that contains a clause providing for re-assignment upon repayment. This case questions the effectiveness of the right to compel the reassignment but the court based its decision on the general prohibition against assignment in the lease in a situation where the landlord was unaware of the original assignment as security. *Anjo Restaurant Corp. v. Sunrise Hotel Corp.*, 98 Misc. 2d 597 (N.Y. Sup. Ct., Nassau Cty. 1979). The Maryland Court of Appeals similarly refused to give effect to the exercise of a right to take back the leasehold by a purchase money secured party who had assigned the lease to its purchaser/debtor (with the landlord's consent), citing the landlord's ignorance of the security agreement and lack of consent thereto and emphasizing that the landlord had consented only to an instrument that completely divested the assignor of its leasehold interest. *Italian Fisherman, Inc. v. Middlemas*, 313 Md. 156 (1986). This case is also significant for its discussion of the issue of whether an assignment by an assignee back to an assignor is exempt from a landlord consent requirement. The court cited cases permitting such an assignment without consent, but stated those cases were not widely accepted and that the better approach, which it followed, was to apply such a requirement to an assignment back to the assignor. *Id.* at 166-67.

Logically, there is no reason why a "snap-back" clause in the form provided above should not permit the assignor to bring an action for ejectment based on a breach of a condition subsequent. Such an action was permitted in a case where an instrument of assignment reserved a right of re-entry. *Hammes v. Esposito*, 10 Ill. App. 3d 6 (1st Dist. 1973). *See also Craig v. Summers*, 47 Minn. 189, 193 (1891). However, such a remedy takes time, and would be of little use to an assignor attempting to regain the tenant's position under the lease prior to its termination for default.

As to whether the "snap-back" rights create a sublease, analogy to the cases on assignments with rights to re-entry suggest that they do not, although the courts are divided on this point. *See* 49 Am. Jur. 2d Landlord and Tenant § 1080, and cases cited therein. Significantly, most of these cases involve instruments purporting to be subleases (with the sublandlord having default remedies and rights to re-enter), but which may be deemed assignments because the transferor was found to have transferred its entire leasehold interest. Significantly, these cases arise in the context of whether the transferee is liable to the landlord, which would be the case only if the transfer is an assignment and not a sublease. *See, e.g., Sexton v. Chicago Storage Co.*, 129 Ill. 318 (1889); *St. Joseph & St. L.R. Co. v. St. Louis, I. M. & S. Railway Co.*, 36 S.W. 602 (Mo. 1896). In a case where the instrument of transfer contained language of both assignment and sub-lease, the Texas Supreme Court reached a contrary result, finding that the transferor's reserved rights and stated intention to retain control of the property made the instrument a sublease. *Davis v. Vidal*, 105 Tex. 444 (1912). One court, however, declined to recharacterize an assignment and assumption agreement as a sublease because it contained a "conditional reassignment on breach," distinguishing what it termed a "contingent right of re-entry" in that agreement from the reversionary interest of a sublease. *Nedick's Stores, Inc. v. T.S.N.Y Realty Corp.*, 156 A.D.2d 123 (N.Y. App. Div., 1st Dept. 1989).

The common theme of these cases is that the assignor's right to get the leasehold estate back from the assignee, whether through a right to reassignment of the lease or some form of right of re-entry, resulted in the courts deciding whether the instrument, notwithstanding its characterization by the parties, was really an assignment or a sublease. Therefore, the use of a "snap-back" clause at least raises a question as to whether the instrument is an assignment at all. If it is determined to be a sublease, the parties' positions are that of sublandlord and subtenant, but without sublease clauses dealing with sublease issues.

If the assignee becomes insolvent, it is unlikely that a bankruptcy court would permit a "snap-back" clause to affect the protections afforded a bank-ruptcy trustee or debtor-in-possession under the federal Bankruptcy Code.

The right to assume, reject, or assign the lease provided in Section 365(a) of the Code (11 U.S.C. § 365(a)) in order to preserve the assignee's estate for the benefit of its creditors or facilitate a plan of reorganization presumably would take precedence over an assignor's right of re-assignment, even if enforceable under state law.

[D]   Is the Confusion Worth It?

An assigning tenant's counsel who requests a "snap-back" clause may think he or she has been clever in retaining something in a transaction where his or her client is supposed to be transferring everything. This view is illusory.

Basically, a user of space that requires an assignment in the first place is not likely to agree to a "snap-back" clause for the same reasons it will not agree to a sublease. Control of the space in a direct landlord-tenant relationship will be too important to permit the relationship to be affected by claims of third parties no longer involved. No assignee will agree to put its right to the leased premises (and its ability to conduct its business at the premises) at risk if there is a dispute with the assignor. Perhaps most significantly, the threat of having to re-assign the lease will interfere with attempts to resolve differences with the landlord and put the assignee at a disadvantage in the event of a lease dispute. If the assignor has the bargaining power to obtain the "snap-back" clause, it might as well insist on a sublease.

A demand for re-assignment under a "snap-back" clause could be problematic for the landlord. Landlords want to know who their tenants are and with whom they need to deal if problems arise, and will not want to be caught up in a dispute between the original tenant and the present tenant regarding who has the right to the leasehold. In any event, unless the landlord consents to the "snap-back" provision at the time of the original lease assignment, a re-assignment probably would be subject to general lease restrictions on assignment including recapture rights and requirements for landlord consent, so the assignor may have a right it cannot exercise. *See Italian Fisherman v. Middlemas*, 313 Md. 156 (1986).

With all of these risks and uncertainties, there seems no reason to depart from the use of a normal assignment or sublease, where the rights and obligations of the parties will be set forth in the instrument they choose and the legal consequences determined by recognized rules of law governing the type of arrangement they specifically agreed to.

Finally, as discussed above, the right to re-assignment probably is worthless in the event of the assignee's bankruptcy, the likely scenario where the assignee is defaulting under lease obligations. The assignor remains liable to the landlord under the lease as an agreement between parties not in bankruptcy, and to the extent it pays the landlord its status will be no more than that of an unsecured creditor. The right to a reassignment will not have helped.

CHAPTER 16
COMMON INTEREST OWNERSHIP

Rebecca Fischer

§ 16.01   INTRODUCTION

[C]   Necessary Documents

Page 1000, add to note 21:

See Garden Lakes Community Ass'n v. Madigan, 62 P.3d 983 (Ariz. 2003), where the Arizona Court of Appeals, in light of state statutes promoting the use of solar energy, refused to enforce a restrictive covenant that effectively prohibited a homeowner from installing solar energy devices.

§ 16.02   THE DECLARATION

[B]   Essential Terms

Page 1004, add to note 29:

In one case in Massachusetts, the tax assessor sought to assess, not the condominium project's common area, but instead, the rights to build additional units on that common area. The developer had specifically reserved those development rights in the project documents, and those rights had passed to the owners by operation of law. *See* § **16.10,** main volume and supplement, for a discussion of development rights. Applying Massachusetts statutes that prohibit the separate taxation of condominium common areas, the court rejected the assessor's attempt to sever the development rights from the underlying fee, and to subject the rights to separate taxation. *First Main Street Corp. v. Board of Assessors of Action*, 725 N.E.2d 1076 (Mass. App. Ct. 2000).

In addition, in Colorado, state law (based on UCIOA) prohibits a county tax assessor from taxing common areas as separate property. However, that law does not prevent the county from assessing certain parts of the common areas at separate rates. In *Manor Vail Condominium Ass'n v. Board of Equalization of Eagle County*, 956 P.2d 654 (Colo. Ct. App. 1998), the court confirmed the authority of the county tax assessor to assess certain common elements in a residential complex at a higher rate applicable to commercial properties. The common areas in question included a restaurant and meeting rooms that were open to the general public, and that were not claimed as being integral to the residential use of the individual condominium units.

§ 16.04   THE OWNERS ASSOCIATION — GENERAL POWERS AND DUTIES

[A]   The Role of the Executive Board

Page 1017, add to note 45:

On the basis of the business judgment rule, New York's highest court refrained from interfering with the decision of a cooperative's board to eject a shareholder-tenant for his objectionable conduct. *40 West 67th St. Corp. v. Pullman*, 790 N.E.2d 1174 (N.Y. 2003). The shareholder-tenant had argued that the termination of his relationship with the co-op could rest only on a court's independent evaluation of the reasonableness of the co-op's action, but the court decided that the business judgment standard governed the co-op's decision. The court recounted that the defendant complained about his neighbors, an elderly couple, who had resided in the co-op for more than 20 years. First, the defendant charged falsely that the couple ran a dangerous and illegal business in their apartment. Then the defendant distributed flyers to the building residents variously calling the husband a "psychopath in our midst," falsely accusing the couple of cutting the defendant's telephone lines, and suggesting that the wife had some intimate personal relationship with the wife of the president of the co-op board. In time, the defendant pressed charges that resulted in the arrest of the husband (which charges were subsequently dismissed), and the defendant filed a series of lawsuits against the couple, the cooperative, and its president. The court observed that, despite the deferential standard represented by the business judgment rule, a court should undertake review of board decisions in certain instances, where the aggrieved association member can show that the board acted outside the scope of its

authority, or in a way that did not legitimately further the corporate purpose or in bad faith. However, in this case, given a lease agreement that
expressly provided that termination was a remedy for the shareholder-tenant's
objectionable conduct, and conduct reportedly not just objectionable, but
outrageous, the court readily refused to review the board's decision.

Page 1018, add to text after note referent 50:

New Jersey is one of the states subscribing to the old rule. Under the New
Jersey Condominium Act, a condominium association may sue the devel-
oper for construction defects related to the common elements, and a unit
owner may sue the developer for defects within the unit. *Society Hill
Condominium Ass'n, Inc. v. Society Hill Assocs.*, 347 N.J. Super. 163, 789
A.2d 138 (2002). *See also Mitchell v. LaFlamme (v. American Housing
Foundation and the Courtyards of Baytown Owners Ass'n)*, 60 S.W.3d 123
(Tex. App. — Houston 2002, no writ). Addressing the claims of owners in
a townhome project established with the project association as the owner
of the common areas, the Texas Court of Appeals held that recovery for
damages to the common areas belonged exclusively to the association.
Accordingly, the townhome owners had no individual contract or property
right in the common areas for which they could sue for damages, but were
required instead to bring a derivative suit on behalf of the association.

Page 1019, add to note 51:

In *Yacht Club II Homeowners Ass'n v. A.C. Excavating*, No. 02CA0645
(Colo. Ct. App., Nov. 30, 2003), a townhome association had sued various
subcontractors, alleging negligence in the construction of both the individual units and common areas, with the result of heaving basement
floors, cracking concrete foundations, reverse sloping driveways, leaking
windows and doors, slanted floors, damaged drywall, water penetration of
the roofs, and deteriorating exterior trim. The trial court granted summary
judgment against the association on grounds that the association lacked
standing to pursue claims for construction defects to individual townhome
units. The Colorado Court of Appeals reversed, citing the Colorado
Common Interest Ownership Act, which expressly permits an association
to bring an action on its own behalf and also on behalf of two or more unit
owners, provided the matter is one "affecting the common interest community." As the townhome units in this case were part of the common
interest community, the association met the statutory conditions for filing
suit on behalf of unit owners.

[B]   Administration of the Common Elements

Page 1023, add to note 56:

At least one case illustrates the pitfalls for the developer and the association members when the documents leave doubt regarding the extent of the property to be administered by the association once the developer is no longer on the scene. In *Poblette v. Towne of Historic Smithville Community Ass'n*, 809 A.2d 178 (N.J. Super. Ct., App. Div. 2002), the governing documents established easements for the present and future installation of utilities and storm water systems, among other infrastructure improvements. The developer went bankrupt, and over time, storms demonstrated the inadequacies of a detention basin in the subdivision that had been intended for flood control. Owners in the development sued the association, alleging the association, as holder of an easement carrying control of the common facility, had a duty to maintain the basin. The association sought to avoid the easement and the responsibility with arguments including a failure by the developer to pass control of the common area to the association. In the lower court and on appeal, the association lost. Although the developer's bankruptcy prevented a formal transfer of the basin area from the developer to the association, the court found sufficient indications in the governing documents that the common areas were planned for ultimate ownership by the association, and so the transition was deemed to have occurred at the time of the developer's bankruptcy.

[D]   Power to Make Rules

Page 1027, add to note 62:

See also Woodside Village Condominium Ass'n, Inc. v. Jahren, 806 So. 2d 452 (Fla. 2002), cited in note 154 of this chapter, main volume, for a case upholding an amendment to a condominium declaration passed by the required majority vote, restricting the right to lease a unit in the project, not to enhance the project's qualifications for secondary mortgage market financing, but simply to avoid the perceived negative impact of absentee owners on the quality of life in the development and the market value of the units.

The decision in *Mulligan v. Panther Valley Property Owners Ass'n*, 766 A.2d 1186 (N.J. Super. Ct. App. Div. 2001), highlights several points in the debate on rules pitting the rights of the individual against the desires of the common interest community. In the wake of New Jersey's passage

of "Megan's Law" (requiring that persons convicted of sex offenses register their names and addresses in public records), the members of the
Panther Valley Property Owners Association adopted an amendment to
their project declaration and their association bylaws, prohibiting any
individual registered as a "Tier 3" offender under Megan's Law (the classification assigned to a person considered at highest risk of committing
repeat offenses) from residing in the Panther Valley community. Although
the appellate court refused to rule on a homeowner's challenge to the
Megan's Law rule (for want of a sufficient record in the trial court),
the court did not refrain from discussing the merits of the arguments. First,
the court decided that a judicial review of a New Jersey community association's rule should be based on a "reasonableness" standard (in contrast
to a less stringent "business judgment rule" standard). In making that
determination, the court noted that the rule in dispute surfaced in an
amendment to the community's governing documents, as opposed to the
original project documents in place when the plaintiff owner bought her
Panther Valley residence. For that reason, the court viewed the new rule as
not entitled to the strong presumption of validity sometimes accorded
restrictive covenants in place at the beginning of the project. Further
justifying the reasonableness standard in reviewing the rule, the court
noted that the amendment was passed (in accordance with the governing
documents) by a simple majority vote, and not with substantial majority
approval, which the court considered a more widely accepted procedure in
community association practice.

Turning to the homeowner plaintiff's specific complaints, the court
quickly dismissed arguments that the Megan's Law rule infringed on the
owner's right to alienate her property. The effect of the rule was equal
against all owners in the project, and the effect was also apparently
insignificant, in light of the very small number of individuals disqualified
from purchasing in the project because of the rule. However, the court
worried more about the public policy implications of such a rule, if communities across the state were to adopt comparable versions and make
housing inaccessible to Tier 3 registrants.

§ 16.05   THE OWNER'S USE OF THE COMMON ELEMENTS

Page 1030, add to note 67:

One case demonstrates the importance of protecting the rights of the owners to keep the common elements truly common, for use by all. In *Dobbs v.
Knoll*, 92 S.W.3d 176 (Mo. Ct. App. 2002), three landowners filed suit

against the trustees of their homeowners' association to quiet title to the property behind their lots. The parcels in dispute had been labeled on the plat as "community area and common easement," and apparently the trustees held fee ownership of the parcels. In the case of one of the landowner plaintiffs, the land in question was located within the fenced area demarcating an owner's back yard, and the owner was told, when he purchased the lot, that he owned the land to the back fence. The association trustees discovered the mistake and demanded that the landowner relocate the fence to exclude the common area, but did nothing to enforce the demand. The other landowners extended the boundaries of their yards to include the disputed area, and improved it with features such as landscaping and irrigation, and in one instance, hedges that impeded access to the parcel by other owners. In the quiet title action, the Missouri court rebuffed the association trustees' claims that the use had been permissive and found that the landowners "had exceeded a reasonable exercise of their right to use the common ground" and more, had established the elements of adverse possession.

§ 16.06   THE OWNER'S LOT

Page 1032, add to note 69:

Compare Terrien v. Zwit, 467 Mich. 56, 648 N.W.2d 602 (2002), holding that covenants permitting only residential uses, and expressly prohibiting commercial, industrial or business uses, preclude the operation of a family day care home, and a covenant precluding such an operation is not unenforceable as violating Michigan public policy. The Michigan Supreme Court distinguished the case from another decision by the Michigan Court of Appeals, which had determined that a family day care home did *not* violate a subdivision covenant that permitted only residential uses. The higher court reasoned that a covenant like the one at issue in *Terrien*, barring any commercial or business enterprises, was broader in scope than a more briefly worded covenant permitting only residential uses.

§ 16.07   DESIGN REVIEW

Page 1035, add to note 76:

In *Pagosa Lakes Property Owners Ass'n, Inc. v. Caywood*, 973 P.2d 698 (Colo. App. 1998), the association had sought a mandatory injunction requiring the removal of a manufactured home from an owner's lot. The manufactured home did not comply with the Uniform Building Code, in violation of standards set forth in unrecorded rules adopted by the board of directors after the defendant owners had purchased their lot. The subdivision predated Colorado's adoption of the Common Interest Ownership Act ("CIOA," the state's version of UCIOA), but among the CIOA sections that apply retroactively to pre-CIOA subdivisions are provisions that authorize an association to adopt and amend rules and regulations. The defendants argued that the association exceeded its authority in adopting and enforcing unrecorded restrictions on the property, but the court upheld the injunction. The court reasoned that the project declaration, which was recorded for the subdivision before the defendants' lot purchase, created broad powers in the association and the project's architectural review committee, and the purchasers were charged with notice of those powers and also with notice of the provisions of CIOA that governed the subdivision retroactively. Accordingly, the court declined to hold that the requirement for compliance with the Uniform Building Code could not be enforced unless the requirement was separately recorded in the public records.

§ 16.08   ASSESSMENTS BY THE ASSOCIATION

Page 1045, add to note 88:

The decision in *Linden Condominium Ass'n, Inc. v. McKenna*, 726 A.2d 502 (Conn. 1999), illustrates the importance of an association's timely collection of delinquent assessments, to avoid loss of dues more than six months in arrears. The Connecticut Supreme Court, interpreting state law modeled on UCIOA, held that a condominium association could not seek a deficiency judgment as part of its foreclosure action enforcing its priority lien for six months' amount of assessments, where the first mortgage redeemed the foreclosed unit by paying the association's priority claim. However, the court did permit the association to bring a wholly separate suit to recover the remaining assessment charges owed to the association.

Page 1045, add to note 89:

See Longanecker v. Diamondhead Country Club, 760 So. 2d 764 (Miss. 2000). The project covenants that required all assessments to be applied to each lot on an *equal* basis did not prevent the association from imposing different rates of assessments for security services on an *equitable* basis, depending on whether the lots in question were improved or unimproved. In *Bankler v. Vale*, 75 S.W.3d 29 (Tex. App. — San Antonio 2001, *reh'g overruled*), the Texas Court of Appeals held that the trial court did not abuse its discretion in issuing an injunction against a condominium board of directors that sought to impose special assessments to build a reserve account and to fund emergency improvements, in light of governing documents that did not go that far in granting the board authority to deal with even pressing capital improvements. The condominium declaration specifically limited the board's authority to impose assessments for capital additions and improvements to circumstances expressly provided by the declaration, and the declaration denied that authority except as necessary to cover unforeseen emergency expenses. As the board intended the assessments in question to pay for deferred capital maintenance expenses, and not immediate, urgent repairs, the appellate court upheld the lower court's injunction, and refused to substitute the board's action, no matter how reasonable, for the unambiguous limitations of the project declaration and bylaws.

§ 16.10   RIGHTS OF THE DECLARANT

Page 1066, add to note 102:

The decision, *Arrowhead by the Lake Ass'n, Inc. v. Arrowhead by the Lake, Inc.*, 2000 WL 33124430 (Conn. Super. 2000), details exactly what a condominium developer should not attempt in a last ditch, unilateral modification of the project documents. One day before the expiration of the developer control period contemplated under the original declaration, the developer recorded an amended declaration that purported to extend and expand the developer's right to build out the property, change the unit boundaries, and lower the voting approval requirements for changes to the use restrictions governing the units. The court issued a permanent injunction against the developer's implementation of the amendment, together with a decree vesting title in the condominium property in the unit owners, free and clear of the declarant's development rights.

Page 1069, add to note 120:

In jurisdictions without the statutory limitations imposed by UCIOA or the Uniform Condominium Act on the rights of the developer to direct the project association by making appointments to the board, courts may still restrict the developer's control to the start-up phases crucial to the development and marketing of the project. *See Unrau v. Kidron Bethel Retirement Servs., Inc.*, 27 P.3d 1 (Kan. 2001).

Page 1070, add to note 123:

The consequences of ignoring these guidelines were the subject of *Chesus v. Watts*, 967 S.W.2d 97 (Mo. Ct. App. 1998). The court used principles drawn from the state's Uniform Condominium Act and contract law to address claims of lot purchasers in a planned unit development. The court applied the doctrine of promissory estoppel to hold that the association had standing to sue the developer for the developer's failure to complete and deliver to the association the common area improvements that the developer had promised in return for the premium prices paid by the subdivision buyers.

§ 16.12 ENFORCEMENT OF THE DECLARATION

Page 1084, add to note 141:

A Pennsylvania case presented one court with an opportunity to confirm the power and validity of an attorneys' fees clause in a project declaration, when a homeowner who resisted a $1,200 assessment wound up paying the assessment and, in addition, more than $46,000 for attorneys' fees spent by the association in collecting the delinquent payment. *Mountain View Condominium Ass'n v. Bomersbach*, 734 A.2d 468 (Pa. Commw. Ct. 1999). The homeowner's case was not helped by the facts that the initial tally of attorneys' fees sought by the association with the first demand for payment was only $500, and that the docket in the case revealed a homeowner defendant "who engaged in trench warfare" in fighting the assessment. *See also Bitting v. Central Pointe Condominium Bd. of Managers*, 970 S.W.2d 898 (Mo. Ct. App. 1998).

Page 1085, add to note 142:

See Ridgewood Homeowners Ass'n v. Mignacca, 813 A.2d 965 (R.I. 2003), where evidence of just a few violations, in a subdivision of over 70 families, of a covenant prohibiting residents from maintaining structures to house animals, did not suggest changes to the subdivision property that were so radical and permanent as to justify abandoning the restriction and waiving the association's right to enforce it.

Page 1085, add to note 143:

In *Ferrary v. Behan*, 25 Conn. L. Rptr. 408 (Conn. Super. Ct. 2001), a real estate agency and real estate broker were allowed to enforce Connecticut's version of the UCIOA. The plaintiffs were not owners, but instead, agents for owners in the project. The brokers won damages for commissions lost when sales of condominium units in the project, listed by the plaintiffs, were derailed by the project association's failure to deliver to the prospective purchasers the disclosures in the form of a resale certificate required by the state's Act. As the brokers fit the definition of persons adversely affected by the association's noncompliance with the Act, they were entitled to remedies under the Act.

In a different twist on the question, at least one court has cast doubt on a developer's attempt to limit lawsuits against it. In an unreported decision, a federal district court in Indiana denied a developer's motion for judgment on the pleadings, allowing the plaintiffs to continue to argue that a covenant in a declaration, prohibiting a suit against the developer or the association for any failure to carry out the declaration on any claim other than negligence or unworkmanlike construction or services, was unconscionable. *Tomlinson v. Village Oaks Dev. Co.*, 2003 WL 21180644 (S.D. Ind. 2003).

§ 16.13   DURATION, AMENDMENT, AND TERMINATION OF THE DECLARATION

Page 1089, add to note 154:

The Florida Supreme Court, in a jurisdiction that has not embraced UCIOA, has decided that an amendment to a condominium declaration, adopted in compliance with the procedures for amendment set forth in the declaration, may restrict the right of an owner in the project to lease his unit by prohibiting such a lease entirely within the first year of ownership, and by limiting leases in subsequent years to a duration of nine months in any one-year period. *Woodside Village Condo. Ass'n, Inc. v. Jahren*, 806 So. 2d 452 (Fla. 2002). The court rejected the plaintiff's arguments that the restriction was unreasonable, arbitrary, and capricious and was essentially confiscatory, and upheld the amendment for several reasons. First, Florida courts have recognized that condominium living is unique, as it typically involves more restrictions upon the rights of the individual unit owners than owners of rental apartments or single-family residences. Second, Florida's statutory scheme and the declaration in this particular case permitted the condominium owners to amend the declaration on a wide variety of issues. Finally, the court noted that the majority of courts in other jurisdictions have held that a duly adopted modification that restricts occupancy or leasing will bind owners who purchased their units before the amendment became effective, and the court added its decision to the majority rule. The owners were charged with knowledge of the statute and the declaration allowing amendments, and so the court decided the amendments were valid and enforceable.

Page 1089, add to note 156:

For an example of a case requiring that an amendment to a project's protective covenants conform to the general plan of the development, *see West v. Evergreen Highlands Ass'n*, 55 P.3d 151 (Colo. App. 2001). The Colorado Court of Appeals held that, as a matter of first impression, restrictive covenants could not be amended pursuant to a covenant provision allowing 75 percent of the owners to modify the covenants, to add new restrictions regarding matters not addressed in the existing covenants. In particular, the court struck down new covenants binding all owners in the subdivision to be members of an association, to pay dues to the association, and to subject their lots to liens for non-payment of the dues. The Colorado Supreme Court has granted certiorari.

Page 1090, add to note 157:

A Colorado case adopts and illustrates the principles promoted in the Restatement. In *Evergreen Highlands Ass'n v. West*, 73 P.3d 1 (Colo. 2003), the developer had created a subdivision before the state's adoption in 1992 of statutes based on UCIOA. The subdivision documents included a declaration that provided for an association to own and maintain a park that was open to all residents and almost entirely surrounded by the subdivision lots. The original covenants did not require the lot owners to be members of the association or to pay dues, but the association's articles did recite functions that included paying taxes on the common area, maintaining the common area, and determining annual fees. The declaration contained a clause permitting a change or modification to the restrictions upon the vote of owners of at least 75 percent of the lots in the development, and in 1995, the owners used that procedure to adopt an amendment that required all the lot owners to be members and pay assessments, enforceable with liens imposed by the association. This case resulted when one dissenting homeowner sued to challenge the validity of the amendment, arguing that the changes contemplated under the amendment procedures did not encompass the wholesale modifications adopted here. The Colorado Supreme Court disagreed and went farther, citing the Restatement and holding that, even in the absence of an express covenant mandating the payment of assessments, this association had the implied power to levy assessments as necessary to carry out its duty, as indicated by the articles of incorporation, to maintain the common areas described on the subdivision plat.

Where the assessment powers of an association are expressly and specifically limited, however, there is no room to imply that the association has authority to breach those limits. In *Quinn v. Castle Park Ranch Property Owners Ass'n*, 77 P.3d 823 (Colo. Ct. App. 2003), the covenants provided that the association could levy assessments for common expenses generally in a maximum amount of $300 in any year. Nonetheless, the association members met and voted in favor of a $17,000 special assessment for costs of paving a private road in the subdivision, and the assenting owners signed a supplemental declaration subjecting their property to the obligation to pay the additional charge. Some homeowners who had dissented from the vote then declined to sign the supplemental declaration, refused to pay the assessment, and sued for a declaratory judgment that the association had exceeded its authority in making the levy. Reasoning that judges should enforce the plain language of a covenant that is clear on its face, the court refused to enforce the additional assessment against the dissenting members.

CHAPTER 17
BANKRUPTCY

James R. Stillman

§ 17.01   AN INTRODUCTION TO BANKRUPTCY COUNSELING

[C]   The Eclectic Sources of Bankruptcy

Page 1103, add after carryover sentence at top of page:

The authorized number of bankruptcy courts in the United States is found in 28 U.S.C. § 152(a)(2).

[D]   What Happens to the Other Side When a Bankruptcy Case Is Commenced?

Page 1103, add to note 4:

28 U.S.C. § 152(a)(1) has been revised to provide for 14-year terms for bankruptcy judges.

Page 1104, add to note 7:

The automatic stay even prevents *enforcing* a claim against the debtor that the bankruptcy court itself awarded during the bankruptcy case. *See Temecula v. LPM Corp. (In re LPM Corp.)*, 269 B.R. 217 (B.A.P. 9th Cir. 2001).

Page 1106, replace note 24:

[24] 11 U.S.C. §§ 363(f) (power of bankruptcy court to sell free of liens); 361(e) (right of creditor to demand adequate protection).

Page 1107, add to note 30:

Notwithstanding *LaSalle*, bankruptcy lawyers have proven relentless and creative in trying to formulate real estate plans under which the existing owners keep control. *See, e.g., Beal Bank, S.S.B. v. Waters Edge Ltd. Partnership*, 248 B.R. 668 (D. Mass. 2000).

§ 17.02   THE PURCHASE AND SALE AGREEMENT

[A]   Counseling the Purchaser Regarding Bankruptcy

[3]   Risk to Purchaser's Investments in Improvements

Page 1111, add at end of second bullet:

The escrow agreement itself is an executory contract that the debtor can almost always break. *See generally* Byrne, "Escrows and Bankruptcy," 48 Bus. Law. 761 (1993).

[8]   When the Seller Is the Master Developer

Page 1114, note 41, correct citation for **Garfinkel** *article:*

28 Real Prop. Prob. & Tr. J. 82 (1993).

[B]   Counseling the Seller Regarding the Risks Associated With a Buyer's Bankruptcy

[2]   How Sellers Try to Draft "Exceptions" to Assignability

Page 1116, add to third paragraph:

Experienced practitioners expect that any clause in a commercial real estate contract that purports to require performance solely by an existing party will be attacked under 11 U.S.C. § 365(e)(1), which nullifies so-called *ipso facto* clauses in bankruptcy. *See, e.g., Crow Dev. Ltd. Partnership v. Jamboree LLC (In re Crow Winthrop Operating Partnership)*, 241 F.3d 1121 (9th Cir. 2001) ("change of ownership" prohibition rendered ineffective).

[4] No Automatic Way to Terminate Contract Once Bankruptcy Intervenes

Page 1117, add to second paragraph:

An automatic price escalation clause was found to be "bankruptcy neutral" and therefore enforceable against the debtor in *Yates Dev. Inc. v. Old Kings Interchange, Inc. (In re Yates Development Inc.)*, 256 F.3d 1285 (11th Cir. 2001).

§ 17.06   THE LEASE

[A] Bankruptcy Checklist for Representing the Tenant

Page 1130, add new bullet at end of subsection [A]:

- The tenant has a very strong position should the debtor/landlord have assumed the lease formally during the case, then elect to breach. This happens most commonly when a liquidation trustee is appointed after the reorganization effort fails. *See, e.g., Einstein/Noah Bagel Corp. v. Smith (In re BCE West, L.P.)*, 264 B.R. 578 (B.A.P. 9th Cir. 2001) (discussing the scope of the "administrative claim" such a tenant enjoys in the case).

[B] Bankruptcy Checklist for Representing the Owner/Lessor

Page 1130, add to text after note 66:

But insofar as the automatic stay will not toll the mere running out of time, where state law provided for a truly self-executing lease termination effective some number of days after the service of a notice of termination, and the notice was served pre-petition, then all rights of the debtor in the premises were extinguished and the lease could not be administered in bankruptcy, even when the period ran out after the case was commenced. *Policy Realty Corp. v. Treber Realty LLC*, 2000 WL 534265 (2d Cir. May 2, 2000) (New York law; unpublished opinion); and *see* note 81 main volume, and accompanying text.

Page 1130, add after note 66:

- This includes any right to spend or apply the security deposit, insofar as the deposit consists of money or other property posted by the tenant. In bankruptcy law, the landlord's rights in the security deposit will be deemed a *security interest in* "property of the estate," and therefore the automatic stay will apply. *See United States v. Whiting Pools, Inc.*, 462 U.S. 198, 207 (1983).

- In most cases, the bankruptcy filing will not prevent the landlord from suing third-party lease guarantors or from having access to other third-party credit enhancement instruments, such as letters of credit, because third parties are generally not protected by the automatic stay in the tenant's case. *See, e.g., Kopolow v. P.M. Holding Corp. (In re Modern Textile, Inc.)*, 900 F.2d 1184 (8th Cir. 1990); *In re Page*, 18 B.R. 713 (D.D.C. 1982) (rejecting contrary aberrant analysis of *In re Twist Cap, Inc.*, 1 B.R. 284 (Bankr. M.D. Fla. 1979)); *Arden v. Hotel Partners (In re Arden)*, 176 F.3d 1226 (9th Cir. 1999). Is a landlord therefore better off, from the bankruptcy point of view, to take a letter of credit and *not* cash for the security deposit? At least one commentator thinks so, Anton N. Natsis, "When Lease Is More," 23 L.A. Law. 46, 48–49 (No. 10 Jan. 2001), while the traditional advice is for the landlord to take cash, as much as can be gotten, *see, e.g.,* Misha D. Weidman, "Negotiating Commercial Leases," CEB Action Guide 38 (Spring 1993).

Other recent cases involving the landlord's access to third-party letters of credit (while the tenant is in bankruptcy) include *In re Farm Fresh Supermarkets of Maryland, Inc.*, 257 B.R. 770 (Bankr. D. Md. 2001); *In re Hechinger Investment Inc.*, 2001 Bankr. LEXIS 148 (D. Del. Jan. 29, 2001). The bankruptcy court enjoined the landlord from drawing on the letter of credit, where the tenant's only default under the lease was filing the bankruptcy case. *In re Metrobility Optical Sys., Inc.*, 268 B.R. 326 (Bankr. D.N.H. 2001).

Page 1131, add to note 71:

The landlord's reasonable attorneys' fees will also be included in the cure price, in most cases. *See In re Crown Books Corp*, 269 B.R. 12 (Bankr. D. Del. 2001).

Page 1132, add to note 77:

Yet the trend in bankruptcy is decidedly against enforcement of lease recapture or profit-sharing clauses, however artfully drafted. *See South Coast Plaza v. Standor Jewelers West, Inc. (In re Standor Jewelers West, Inc.)*, 129 B.R. 200, 202 (B.A.P. 9th Cir. 1991) (enforcing an "allocation provision" in the lease would not be permitted because it would "adversely affect the ability of the [tenant] in its rehabilitation effort"); *see also*, for a thorough discussion with all the current citations, *In re Boo.Com North America Inc.*, 2000 Bankr. LEXIS 1559 (Bankr. S.D.N.Y. Dec. 15, 2000) (not for publication).

Page 1133, add to note 79:

Centerpoint Properties v. Montgomery Ward Holding Co. (In re Montgomery Ward Holding Corp.), 268 F.3d 205 (3d Cir. 2001) (rejecting proration approach; obligation to pay rent arises for purposes of 11 U.S.C. § 365(d)(3), when the duty to perform arises under the terms of the lease).

Page 1133, add to text after note 80:

Unless the debtor formally rejects the lease in bankruptcy, the debtor's obligation to pay rent post-petition on a lease of commercial real property may continue even where the debtor surrendered possession before commencing bankruptcy. This happens when the landlord "accepted the keys" but expressly did not intend to terminate the lease (consistent with an election regarding remedies). *See, e.g., In re CHS Electronics, Inc.*, 265 B.R. 339 (Bankr. S.D. Fla. 2001).

[C] Synthetic Leases and Other Financing Leases

Page 1134, add to note 84:

See also In re Greenfield Dry Cleaning & Laundry, Inc., 249 B.R. 634 (Bankr. E.D. Pa. 2000) (a settlement agreement in which the lease was continued for some period of time was styled as a "license" and therefore cost the landlord its priority right to rent payments).

§ 17.07   THE REAL ESTATE SECURED LOAN

[B]   Commonly Asked Questions About Loan Documents in Bankruptcy

Page 1138, add to note 95:

The correct view, even in a "title theory jurisdiction," is that the rental assignment creates only a lien. *See Cavros v. Fleet Nat'l Bank (In re Cavros)*, 262 B.R. 206 (Bankr. D. Conn. 2001).

Page 1139, add to note 98:

In addition, a non-consensual sale pre-confirmation, *i.e.*, during the pendency of the bankruptcy case, is not uncommon. *See* 11 U.S.C. § 363(f)(3) (sale by bankruptcy court of property allowed where objecting party holds only a lien).

Page 1140, add to note 103:

The need for the lender unequivocally to have *given notice* of its intent to collect default rate interest, in order to have a claim for default rate interest in bankruptcy, was the subject of *Beal Bank v. Crystal Properties (In re Crystal Properties)*, 268 F.3d 743 (9th Cir. 2001).

Page 1141, add to note 108:

A yield-maintenance fee was recently disallowed by the bankruptcy court in *In re Schwegmann Giant Supermarkets Partnership*, 264 B.R. 823 (Bankr. E.D. La. 2001).

Page 1142, add to note 111:

So, for example, a statutory right to attorneys' fees equal to 15 percent of the loan principal under Georgia law was not allowed in bankruptcy as part of the secured claims. *Royal v. Welzel (In re Welzel)*, 260 F.3d 1284, *mod. on rehearing* en blanc, 275 F.3d 1308 (11th Cir. 2001).

INDEX

References are to sections.